D0709486

BUILDING
WISDOM'S
HOUSE

BUILDING WISDOM'S HOUSE

A Book of Values for Our Time

Bonnie Menes Kahn

Rabbi Stephen S. Pearce

Father John P. Schlegel

Bishop William E. Swing

ADDISON-WESLEY

Reading, Massachusetts

Many of the designations used by manufacturers and sellers to distinguish their products are claimed as trademarks. Where those designations appear in this book and Addison-Wesley was aware of a trademark claim, the designations have been printed in initial capital letters.

Copyright © 1997 by Bonnie Menes Kahn, Stephen S. Pearce, John P. Schlegel, and William E. Swing

All rights reserved. No part of this publication may be reproduced, stored in a retrieval system, or transmitted, in any form or by any means, electronic, mechanical, photocopying, recording, or otherwise, without the prior written permission of the publisher. Printed in the United States of America.

ISBN 0-201-13294-X

Addison-Wesley is an imprint of Addison Wesley Longman, Inc.

Jacket design by Suzanne Heiser
Text design by Karen Savary
Set in 11-point Weiss by dix!

1 2 3 4 5 6 7 8 9—DOH—0100999897
First printing, October 1997

Find us on the World Wide Web at http://www.aw.com/gb/

CONTENTS

❧

I

Setting Out

This is a book about traditional Western Judeo-Christian values. There are other traditions. There are other values. Some of these other traditions deserve to be better known. Why not write about them? Isn't there already a whole world of books about Judeo-Christian values, whole libraries full? Yes. And that is why we write. So many speakers have said they speak for us. So many Americans have claimed to fly that flag. So many writers have tried to sweeten selfish words with sentiment they call religious. And the reader, any reader, you, reader, wonders, "Can that really be so? Am I heir to a tradition that would put me at war with my own neighbors? I am just an ordinary soul. What is it exactly that my own religion is trying to tell me?" Read this book and remember.

RECENT DAYS HAVE SEEN A RESURGENT INTEREST IN religion, especially religion as a public voice. This happens in cycles. One person may be constant and devout and another a skeptic no matter what the setting; just so, religion has its fashions, too. An age is called Scientific or Enlightened, another age turns to moral authority. The skeptic of a pious age, the believer in an age of disbelief, these exist, although uneasily. Through these fashions religion has endured. If we are to learn anything, if we can conclude anything from this long history, we must ask honestly: When has the voice of religion been for the good? When has religion served humankind? And when has religious authority been misused, misguided?

Religion used as the voice of hate is religion misused. History

4 BUILDING WISDOM'S HOUSE

has shown us that. Religion used to condemn imagined conspiracies is religion at its ugliest. Religion used to attack other religions—we have seen it, and it has caused pain and suffering. So when a religious leader talks of conspiracies and his followers declare their fight for a Christian America, when politicians proclaim a cultural war and suggest deporting American citizens, when school prayer leaves the realm of conscience to become a political litmus test, this is not just a newly religious age. This is religion misused. This is religion as a voice of hate.

Each word of hate rings like a shot (some are followed by shots), and the words come rapid fire. The speed is mesmerizing. A phrase, a dare, repeats and ricochets on the news, on the street. So when we sat down to ask ourselves if the voice of religion could bring a message of something better, we thought slowly. We thought long term. We thought in stories and parables, in sermons. We thought over long, long traditions and asked ourselves, where have we been and where are we bound? How can we counter the consequences of hard, fast language thrown at high speed from moving microphones? What can we say to once again put religion in the service of our better impulses?

The very first thing is to assert that we believe in something. Of all the ideas the fundamentalist Right has tried to promulgate, the most dangerous is that those who don't agree with them have no beliefs at all. On the contrary, most of us share some pretty basic ideas about human decency. Why has the word *values* come to mean reactionary politics or personal intolerance? We all hold values; not all Americans shout equally loudly. We all believe in something. In fact, some of these beliefs are exceptionally strong. The belief in equality inspired a generation to fight for civil rights in the face of vicious dogs, in the haze of tear gas. Not all beliefs need be so dramatic, though. Many Americans still believe in the goodness of those around them. They smile and say good morning and don't stop to look at the skin color of those around them. They value human decency. Many Americans pray. They dream quietly of a better world. How did the political and religious fringe come to claim the mantle of Judeo-Christian tradition?

Our second task is to reclaim our shared tradition openly and in a public voice. We will talk about morality, but we will not mean enforced conformity. We will talk about spiritual life, but we will not mean self-righteous self-congratulation. And the words? You won't need a code. Any words are fine. Any words you remember, any words that strike you, any words we offer—take them. The values in this book, the ideas behind this journey, belong to anyone who will claim them. This is the biggest difference between our Judeo-Christian tradition and the one claimed by religious isolationists. The spirit, in their view, can take only one form and is so easily corrupted that they can allow no differences. No doubts. No new influences or old friendships. No halfway steps. But we are here to share. Religion will serve our better impulses when it shows us how to approach other people in a better spirit, not how to run away from them.

STORIES

Religion has a way of showing us how to approach other people. It does so through stories. Mostly we use the Bible as our source and the scriptural tradition of storytelling as our guide. Judeo-Christian tradition is Biblical tradition. The first five books of the Bible make up the Jewish Torah, the text Jews have traditionally believed was revealed by God. This is not the entire Hebrew Bible, or Old Testament, as Christians call it, which includes the words of prophets, psalms, and other writings.

Christians have traditionally believed the New Testament to

be the revelation of Jesus' ministry, His divinity, and God's message of love and redemption. Protestants, especially, turn to scripture for guidance, rather than to the traditions of church organization or structure. But even more than Europe, even more than Asia or South America, North America relies on the parables, lessons, and stories of the Bible. This is a land spare in cathedrals and sparse in stained-glass windows. This is a country empty of frescoes and barely graced with murals. Pageants are fewer and Puritan influence greater. People settled far from their families and the rituals of togetherness. Americans can be loners. Yet while Americans look a million different ways and there is no way to look American, you can imagine almost any American alone with a Bible and the picture fits. The tradition of the family Bible transcends sect or religion or even region. Although the southern United States is sometimes called the Bible Belt because of its intensely Protestant, scripture-based Christianity, the Biblical tradition of storytelling is present everywhere in the United States.

Throughout this book you will read the beliefs and values we share in this Bible tradition. Not all of them are from the Bible. Many of the beliefs and values we hold result from years of Bible study or reflection on the Bible, or simply lives lived in its shadow. Some may be interpretations evolved over many years, or interpretations in light of historical events. This is not a scholarly Biblical exegesis. We are not using America to understand the Bible, but our common Bible wisdom to understand America. This is an essay about America. Our Biblical references are not scholarly, but a kind of common wisdom and paraphrase; same with the prayers. So in our attempt to speak with the common voice, we have written plainly and put some selected sources only at the end. We are not trying to draw distinctions between texts or editions, but to find some common language in order to talk about our traditions. The purpose of sharing traditions is precisely that the review of similarities and differences leads to new meanings, new interpretations, and new understanding of ourselves and our own traditions.

But what is a tradition? For whom do we speak? The ideas contained in these pages are not official doctrine; we cannot even say that all of our coreligionists will agree with us. Tradition does not mean law; far from it. Collective wisdom sounds grand. So here is a formula: we speak for our teachers. A religious tradition is that teacher's voice that taught you who you are. So we will tell you what our teachers taught us, including what they helped us learn for ourselves. Often these lessons were in the form of parables, or from the Jewish commentary called Midrash, which is largely made up of stories, or simply tales about individuals whose experiences serve as examples. We have used this shared tradition to shape our book, with its stories and anecdotes and parables.

We begin each chapter in this book with an individual's dilemma. These anecdotes or stories depict weakness along with strength and, above all, honesty about life's difficulties, even for saints. Saint Julian Hospitator is a tormented soul. Abba Tahnah the Pious, who begins our journey, faces a forced choice. Perhaps he, along with most of us, wants life to be an easier time; we would prefer not to have to weigh our own interests against the interests of others. The Bishop Seabury faces a test of his religious devotion in his need to make a demanding compromise. Lily Kaufman, of the last chapter, has complex and ambivalent feelings about education. She will not hypocritically spout support of an ideal simply for its own sake. These individuals have weaknesses. But the conclusion we draw when we see human weakness is not that people shouldn't hold ideals, not that the divorced shouldn't believe in marriage or that nonbelievers shouldn't support religious hopes. We simply conclude that life's journey takes strength.

The image of the journey suits us. We are people who see our history as wandering, moving, searching for something better. The ancient Hebrews wandered in the desert, and when God instructed them, He said, Leave your home, I will show you a place, a land you do not know, and I will make you my people. God instructed Moses to take the Jews into the desert and out of Egypt. During the journey Moses received the Ten Commandments; Moses himself never settled in the Promised Land. It was on a journey, Mary and Joseph's journey, that the infant Jesus was born in Bethlehem. Jesus told his disciples, Leave your old ways and follow me. It was on a journey, the road to Damascus, that Paul achieved his Christian understanding.

A journey can be a pilgrimage, as it was for many Christians during the Middle Ages, including Chaucer's famous pilgrims in his *Canterbury Tales*. Their journey gave them not only the opportunity to meet others different from themselves but also the leisure to reflect on life, slowly and with humor. We don't call our chapters "The Bishop's Tale" or "The Immigrant's Tale," but we could. Imagine Lily Kaufman and Samuel Seabury sitting together, trading stories and learning from one another. It almost sounds like the beginning of a very funny story. Yet these two have a lot in common: their stamina, their uncertainties, their ornery individualism, their desire to shape the future.

A journey can be an exile, as it was during the Middle Ages for many Jews, who were driven from one country to another. Those travelers carried their beliefs with them from place to place as a source of strength and meaning. Scholars, pilgrims, tradespeople, soldiers, beggars—so many of our historical figures we see in the context of a journey. Saint Ignatius Loyola traveled in pursuit of understanding and godliness. And Gluckl of Hameln, a simple Jewish widow in medieval Germany, traveled to conduct trade and to marry off her children.

In the course of our journey, we make observations and discoveries. In "Crossing Paths," we reflect on our obligations to the human beings around us and how we can best coexist. In "Crossing Rivers" we try to stretch our boundaries: do these rivers hold us in and keep others out, or can we be more inclusive? It is a simple journey of few parts and simply said, but it is over difficult terrain. In the course of our discussion we will see America confront very contemporary questions: immigration, racism, affirmative action, AIDS, environmental pollution, gun control, education. We travel through these subjects as pilgrims, searching, but also as exiles, holding fast to the ideas that give us strength.

And we carry our hope. Journeys all require hope because anger and bitterness won't get you very far. Hope is the essence of the Christian life because the Christian life is essentially prospective, forward looking, a venturing into the unknown. Hope is not static; it is not simply sitting around; it is not passive. But rather like faith and love it is dynamic, a quality of living that ceaselessly moves in the patterns of our lives. Hope in the future is one of the many things we share.

What is more, the journey particularly touches Americans of all religions. It was a journey that brought the ancestors of most of today's Americans to these shores, and then to the frontier as it pushed west. This kind of American journey is inseparable from American optimism, because a journey is a departure into the unknown.

AMERICAN STORIES

In the chapters that follow we take our scriptural storytelling tradition and put it in our own context, for our own time. We write, aware that we are part of a greater religious community. We are, first of all, part of a tradition. We are not the first to join together in this way, and this is not the first time history has demanded such united effort. During the late 1930s and early 1940s American religious leaders stared with alarm at the turmoil in Europe. At a time of growing interfaith initiatives, one initiative in particular stood out as unusual. A Jewish scholar, Louis Finkelstein, asked Protestant and Catholic scholars to join with him to discuss current affairs. The books that he and his coauthors wrote, most notably *Faith for Today* (Town Hall, 1941) and *The Religions of Democracy* (Devin-Adair, 1945), stand as models in their effort to speak with a loud voice by speaking with a united voice.

Some of their concerns echo in our own, and some of their conclusions bear repeating. Perhaps the single strongest message those scholars and theologians had to offer was that the moral individual lives in a social world and shares concerns and obligations with other people. A Jesuit scholar, Gerald Groveland Walsh, S.J., from Fordham University, said that intolerance and personal frustration are two sides of the same coin. The person who hates others is the one who hates himself and, also, the reverse: the person who hates herself will turn that hate on others. Stanley High, writing on behalf of Protestantism, voiced a very beautiful, very American ideal, which he called "social confidence." He described it as the belief that the other fellow, given half a chance, would come through. We've seen it in a million movies. The tough, cynical Humphrey Bogart character, faced with a decision, chooses good. The weak-kneed woman played by Shelley Winters turns out to have a heart of gold. A selfish Harrison Ford selflessly comes through to save the ship. Social confidence is not a personal force; it's a belief in the goodness of others.

These earlier interfaith spokesmen addressed crucial questions of cooperation in wartime and the presence of God in a war-torn world. Frank Kingdon, writing as a Protestant, took special pains to explain that since human beings make political and economic mistakes, human beings must pay the consequences. God, he said, does not make policy, does not dictate policy, and does not draft policy. This was at once a deliberate answer to a world facing Nazi aggression and a defense of religion. As the Hindu Swami Nikhilananda pointed out, it is the political rivalries and bigotries that discredit religion, not religion that fails the decision makers.

Some of these thoughts echo today. Religion looks ugly and discredited when it is seen to be acting as an accomplice to political rivalries and bigotry. But other questions have replaced the questions of that age, and other crises have replaced the crises of that time. When we speak today, we speak to our time, a time of growing fundamentalist fervor.

All over the world religious groups are reaching into their doctine for a stricter, "purer" interpretation. Indian Moslems, Hindus, and Sikhs have hardened their stances toward one another and toward Indian Christians. Religious orthodoxy has gained political power in India and Israel, Algeria and Afghanistan. Moslem religious law is governmentally enforced in Malaysia. The religious dimension in the Serbs' attack on Bosnia and Croatia led to "ethnic cleansing." And if Europe is not close enough for examples of violence with a religious overtone, consider the large number of America's black churches that have recently burned at the hands of a number of individuals and groups who seem to understand the power of religion and the potent symbolism of destroying houses of worship.

America's rising fundamentalism tends to be Christian, and it is part of this growing religious fundamentalism worldwide. This book is our response to our country and our time. There are other countries, there are other responses. Our response, though, has an American flavor.

We live in a religiously pluralist country, where the presence of dozens of denominations and religions contribute to a unique setting, at once filled with religious fervor and overwhelmingly secular. More and more, America has a strong Islamic presence. The future of the country seems to lie in the direction of more interfaith cooperation, more joint effort among Protestant denominations, and more Eastern-oriented worship, including meditation and Buddhist rites. While religion is strong in the United States, Americans on the whole are wary of big institutions, so the laity is a powerful force in American religious practice. Dr. Kahn speaks with the voice of the laity and the voice of secular American society in its dialogue with the clergy.

Bishop Swing speaks from the Episcopal Church of the United States, a Protestant church whose roots lie in the Church of England. Missionaries established Christianity in England in the fourth century of the Common Era. The modern Anglican Church, however, took shape after England's break from the Church of Rome in the sixteenth century. When England began to explore and colonize the North American continent, Anglicans came to settle in America in large numbers. Unlike the Puritans who settled in New England, they were not fleeing religious persecution. But they were seeking a New World and a new chance. They settled largely in the southern colonies, where the Church of England became the official religion in the Carolinas, Maryland, and Virginia. American independence meant independence from the old Church of England and an end to government-sanctioned, official religion. In 1789 American Anglicanism became the Protestant Episcopal Church, separate from the Church of England. As part of the worldwide Anglican Communion, the Episcopal Church recognizes its historical roots.

Approximately 2,500,000 Americans are members. This is a small number compared to the membership of other major Protestant denominations. Unlike the Methodists, Lutherans, Presbyterians, and Baptists, the Episcopalians represent a small, minority denomination. Many worshippers are the descendants of early settlers. Many are the descendants of slaves and slave owners. Many are newcomers. The Church's work is divided into eight provinces with 106 dioceses and missionary districts. A national body, the General Convention, oversees policy. It is composed of a house of bishops and a house of clerical and lay deputies. At the same time, local districts maintain a fair degree of independence. The Episcopal Church mirrors the American government, founded at the same time, with its constitution, its checks and balances, its body of law —and its tensions between national and local opinion.

Episcopal worship and belief focus on the Old and New Testaments of the Bible and the Book of Common Prayer. Scripture and liturgy are important in the Episcopal world. The clergy is an educated clergy, and the worship aims at a this-worldly beauty. Its doctrine is the belief in Jesus Christ as the savior and the incarnation of God. So the physical world, the world of beauty, grace, strength, and glory is part of Episcopal meaning. Like the Roman Catholic Church, it is a church based on sacraments. But unlike the Catholic Church, the Episcopal Church relies not on scripture and tradition alone, but also on reason as a basis of doctrine and worship. The church is hospitable to the full investigation of human truth; its goal is not doctrinal rigidity but an increasing understanding of God in the unfolding story of creation. It is a religion that promotes science as well as the arts. Like the other traditions here, it is an active, engaged religion, dedicated to social action, social concern, and the day-to-day affairs of the world. In American cities the Episcopal Church houses the homeless and provides hospice care; it has been in the forefront of the fight against AIDS. Episcopal missionary work is extensive and its history is long.

Father Schlegel is from the Roman Catholic Church, the oldest and largest of the Christian churches. The Catholic Church is united by government under the Pope in Rome, who is seen as the successor to Jesus' apostle Peter. Jesus entrusted Peter, "the rock upon which I shall found my church," with a ministry of unity and encouragement almost two thousand years ago. The foundation of the church is the teaching of Jesus; its hierarchy of priests, bishops, and cardinals grew from the work of apostles who spread Jesus' message. Throughout the world Catholic worship takes place in neighborhood parishes administered by priests and regional dioceses administered by bishops.

Approximately 60 million Americans are Catholics, or about 22 percent of the American population. These large numbers go along with a long presence on the American continent. Spanish, Portuguese, and French explorers brought Catholicism to the New World five hundred years ago. Spanish priests founded missions in what is now the American Southwest and California. Jesuit priests did missionary work in Canada. English Catholics also settled in the American colonies seeking freedom of worship and wider religious tolerance. Lord Baltimore was one of the early settlers who brought Catholicism to colonial America, and John Carroll signed the Declaration of Independence. John Carroll was the first Roman Catholic bishop in the United States. Although he was actually the bishop of Baltimore, his diocese included the entire country. He was a great advocate of religious liberty and the separation of church and state. A strong promoter of education, he founded Georgetown University and contributed to the growth of the new nation. American Catholics, however, are descendants not only of early settlers, but also of successive waves of immigrants fleeing to a better life: Irish and German, Italian, Czech, Hungarian and Polish, Salvadoran, Mexican, Cuban, Haitian, and Vietnamese.

The essence of Catholic belief is the Nicene Creed, which describes a belief in one God in three persons, the Father, the Son, and the Holy Spirit. Catholics believe that the suffering of Jesus Christ, the Son of God, reveals the nature of sin and the depth of God's love, and that His spirit animates the Church itself. So Church organization and discipline are very important to Catholics. The Church of Rome moves slowly but surely, providing a rocklike consistency in beliefs and principles, as well as a setting for followers to reaffirm these beliefs. The Catholic Church is a guide or source of informed conscience for its members. It sets the guidelines, even though members may follow some rulings closely and others less closely. Within the structure there breathes a centuries-old understanding of human nature. The Catholic Church is a forgiving church whose principles form a moral touchstone for tens of millions of Americans.

Catholicism stresses a very personal, very human experience. Historically the Catholic Church has addressed all dimensions of the wellness of the individual. Parishes are supposed to be personal; the parish priest should know church members. Catholics might feel personally ill at ease if they are at odds with their Church. Catholics may feel personally tied to Jesus or the Virgin Mary or a special saint. Yet for all this intensely personal connection, the overwhelming value is placed on community: community of prayer, of belief, of responsibility.

Within the larger Church, some Catholics join special orders, vowing poverty, chastity, and obedience, and live as nuns, brothers, or priests whose task is to serve the church and the world and assist with the work of the local church. The largest of these Catholic religious orders is the Society of Jesus, founded by Saint Ignatius Loyola and formally approved by Pope Paul III in 1540. Members take a vow of obedience to go wherever the Pope sends them and agree to serve the Church's needs. Father Schlegel is a Jesuit. In the United States, education has become a special mission of the Jesuits, who operate high schools and colleges across the country. The University of San Francisco and Georgetown and Fordham Universities, for example, are Jesuit schools. Jesuit thought has sometimes been a distinctive strand within Catholicism, at once actively serving the world in schools and missions and supporting serious scholarship and intellectual life.

Rabbi Pearce comes from the tradition of Judaism, the religion of the Jews. It has no single head or governing body, yet it is the oldest living religion in the Western world, built on the origins of monotheism perhaps ten millenia ago. The Hebrew tribes of the ancient Near East believed in one God but also codified laws for human conduct, beginning with the Ten Commandments. The Hebrew Bible, the basic book of Jewish belief, is the book that Christians call the Old Testament. The Ten Commandments serve as the first laws of Judaism, Christianity, and Islam.

There are about 7 million Jews in the United States, approximately 2 to 3 percent of the population. They are overwhelmingly the descendants of Ashkenazi, or Western Jews who arrived in the United States after 1881, when European anti-Semitism intensified. There are national organizations and affiliations, schools and seminaries to train rabbis or religious leaders, but worship takes place in individual, local synagogues, and there is no single organization that approves doctrine for all Jews. According to Jewish tradition, religious services may take place wherever ten worshippers, or a minyan, is present, with or without a rabbi. Most American Jews follow one of three versions of Jewish conduct: Orthodox, Conservative, or Reform. Additional groups such as Reconstructionist, Renewal, or Hasidic Jews also offer their own interpretations of Jewish law, ritual, and custom. The tradition here, in this discussion, is filtered through the lens of Reform Judaism, a version of Jewish law and practice heavily reliant on individual conscience and choice and strongly inspired by Enlightenment thought. The Reform movement came out of Germany. Reform synagogues in America, founded by German immigrants, took strong abolitionist stands in the days leading up to the Civil War.

Judaism addresses life's concerns and describes moments of creation, revelation, and redemption, as do other religions, but for the Jew the world as it is now is imperfect. It is the task of human beings to work together with God, as partners in a covenant, to complete the creation of a better world. When that better world is created, the Messiah will come, announcing the Kingdom of God. In this way there is a built-in activism that prompts Jews toward visible roles in society, in order to work toward that more perfect world.

At the same time as it is socially visible, Judaism is home oriented: many celebrations take place in the home, and some religious instruction takes place at home. Jews have survived as a religious group over many centuries with no official church organization and no single doctrine thanks to education and community life.

Jews do not believe that the Messiah has already come, nor do they believe in the divinity of Jesus Christ or of any individual. Holidays are not celebrations of individuals at all. Jewish tradition does not recognize Christmas. This marks Judaism as a minority religion in American life. So Jewish thought is not included here for its large numbers of Jews nor for a large Jewish presence in the direction of American history—neither is true.

Rather, together as representatives of our respective religious groups we seek some shared tradition, something American; we want to see if there is some tradition that can be called Judeo-Christian.

OUR STORY

This book is the fruit of the discussions about American values that the four of us held over the course of a year. Sometimes you'll recognize us as idealists: four people who care deeply about something called society and who want to work to make a better America. We are not against faith. We are against hatred, against bitterness, against the kind of meanness that dehumanizes people. On television and radio people yell at one another; the subject is irrelevant. The yelling is meant to be entertaining. In the political arena, personal attack is the modus operandi. And just as warfare spreads from the battlefield to the civilian population, political attack has turned from other politicians to ordinary citizens. One presidential candidate, when asked about Medicare, attacked his own mother as wasteful and undeserving. People routinely call one another murderers without stopping to see other people's motives, their beliefs—in short, their humanity.

The subject of abortion, possibly the most volatile subject of our day, will appear only briefly in this book. On that subject we are adversaries. Our beliefs cannot be coaxed into a shared statement, beyond reiterating separate arguments and reheating standard disagreements. Since the goal of this book is neither to summarize varying theologies nor to catalogue three political stands, a complete discussion of abortion would not contribute much. There is no shared hope or shared value we can offer beyond this: people believe differently, so make them your adversaries and not your demons. Sometimes there can be no consensus. In that case, fight fairly. Abraham Lincoln used the phrase "With malice toward none." Imagine an America with malice toward none—disagreement, yes, argument, yes, but no malice, no bitterness and hatred. For all of our disagreements and struggles, our shared traditions teach us joy, not rancor. This was one of the conclusions of our discussions: one thing we share is joy.

Can we honestly speak of joy as a shared value? Why would organized religion instruct men and women to be happy? All of us know the darker sides of our own traditions; sometimes it seems as if somber pessimism and disgruntlement are passed out with the prayer books. The trouble is always about to begin, just as it was for the man who walked into a bar one night. "A shot in the glass before the trouble begins," he solemnly demanded of the bartender. "A shot in the glass before the trouble begins," he said again. "A shot in the glass before—" "Wait a minute," the bartender interrupted. "You've been saying that all night. Why don't you stop and pay up?" "Ah," the man intoned, "the trouble is beginning."

What's more, the trouble never ends. In one of his classic Doonesbury comics, Garry Trudeau has two men confiding in one another at an Ivy League college reunion. One man laments that his life has been worthless, he's accomplished nothing, he feels unfulfilled, and the past years have left him disappointed and dissatisfied. His friend tries to sympathize: "I guess the Nobel Prize didn't help then, huh?"

Many of us were raised with an unspoken eleventh commandment: nothing is good enough. A popular joke has it: A grandmother took her grandson to the beach where he was immediately swallowed by the waves and dragged out to sea. The grandmother shrieked and cried, begging God, "Please bring him back, please bring him back." Sure enough, the waves rose, crashed, and delivered the little boy, unharmed, on the shore. The grandmother looked up at the sky and said, "There was a hat."

And on and on. Far from being happy, many of the characters who people our stories and legends and lessons—and our lives— are a miserable lot. It is easy to forget that joy is what has made the whole show go on for hundreds and thousands of years.

Our shared religious tradition derives joy from beauty and values beauty, especially the glory of God's Creation. The Psalms say sing, sing a joyful song. And what beautiful singing we have done. The Gloria of the Catholic Mass is an expression of joy in God, in creation, in life. Religion and its sense of awe is present in two of life's most truly joyful events: birth and marriage. In the Gospel according to Saint John, it was at a marriage, the marriage in Cana, that Jesus' miracles began. The miracle of changing water into wine in that gospel attests to the divinity of Jesus, and it also speaks of the awe and joy of marriage, that experience of transformation from something simple and singular to a compound that is richer and stronger. Marriage is one of life's joyful experiences, perhaps because the prayers are never rote and mindless but always fresh and meaningful to the participants.

Our sad use of one another as objects is not the result of too much joy, but too little. Over and over again we have heard that God surveyed His Creation and saw it as good, but those words seem to have become tired. If we truly believed them, then each unique human being would be cause for joy, having been created in God's image, and no one would be misused or neglected. When we love each child and give each child the care he or she needs, from food and education to constancy and kindness, then we will be living the message of joy in the creation. Babies need to be held and loved individually, intimately. When we treat babies as objects, as part of legislation to punish their parents, we forget their humanity and lose our own. For we lose the chance to see on their faces joy at the world around them.

The Western search for joy through beauty is so much a part of us that we love it, we teach it, and we draw others to it. So there is no need to defend with law the language of Shakespeare. There is no need to force the English language on Americans, any more than there is a need to declare impressionism the officially approved style of painting or Sousa marches our official music. Leaving aside that English is the de facto official language, being necessary for material success, it is also part of America's beauty. And there is no need to define for Americans what is beautiful. Some countries have tried this. But every time a country tries to define beauty politically, the result is politics, not beauty.

OUR SHARED CULTURE DERIVES JOY FROM FREEDOM. There is a sense of lightness and buoyancy when life's burdens are behind you and you live not in worry and fear, but free. It is for this that old men dance. Hasidism, the strain of Judaism founded in the late eighteenth century by Israel ben Eliezer, called the Baal-Shem Tov, stressed joy in God's love. So it was a great compliment when a righteous man was said to have feet so light that he barely touched the ground when he danced. One evening at dinner the Baal-Shem Tov laughed, seemingly for no reason, then again, then he laughed a third time. One of his followers summoned the courage to ask why he laughed, and Baal-Shem Tov said, "Bring here Shabti, the bookbinder, and his wife." He said to Shabti, "Tell us exactly how you spent last Sabbath, Friday night." With some embarrassment Shabti began: "Times have been hard for us. I'll be honest. We had no money for a Shabbat dinner. We didn't even have enough for a smudge of flour. So my wife sat in a dark, cold house while I sat at the shop. I warned her to take nothing of charity. I'll be honest. It was from pride.

"With nothing to cook, and nothing to do, she cleaned every corner three times over and finally went to an old chest to air some old clothes. At the bottom of the chest she found a scrap of an old vest and on it were gold and silver filigree buttons. She took them to the goldsmith, got enough money for candles and food, and set up for the Sabbath.

"In my joy that God provided for us, I took my wife and danced around the room. I'll be honest." Shabti hesitated. "We said the blessings and danced again. We ate and danced again." Shabti looked down, expecting criticism or ridicule. But the Baal-Shem Tov merely turned to his followers and said, "That is why I laughed three times. For the three dances. All of Heaven rejoiced with him and turned round with him in dance." When the world does not weigh heavily, that is joy.

OUR SHARED CULTURE DERIVES JOY FROM TRUTH. The idea of revelation and the experience of seeing, seeing the light, is a source of great elation. Some of the world is hidden, shrouded in a mystery we cannot even begin to fathom. When one part of the mystery becomes clear, we feel the joy of a discovered truth. It is that story of truth hidden and truth revealed that makes the Christian celebration of Epiphany, the revelation of the Christ child, so moving, beautiful, and joyful. The infant Jesus, born in a manger, is unknown, unrecognized. Then the three kings present their gifts, and the truth of history becomes apparent: the people see that God sent this child to change the world; the kings see that their power is inconsequential next to the power of God's divinity. All at once there is realization. This is yet another kind of lightness and buoyancy.

When we say that the feeling of joy has made the whole show go on for thousands of years, that is no exaggeration. The love of joy as beauty has filled our world with magnificent art and music and architecture and literature, not to mention created fashion and molded human relationships. The love of joy as freedom has made us try to lessen our burdens by building economies, realizing our individual wills, and rewarding individual effort. And the love of joy as truth and revelation has made us try harder and harder to understand the world, to build scientific models and technical achievements. If we did not value the elation, the "high" of our experience on earth, we could not have done any of these things. Our shared tradition teaches us joy.

For that reason, when we begin this journey, setting out to discover something about ourselves and our society, we begin with elation and optimism. A world of hatred is a small, uncreative world, and we are looking for something bigger.

This book is a plea for tolerance. Not tolerance at its bare minimum—when people refraining from killing one another, although there's plenty to be said for that. Saying you're for tolerance when all you mean is that you'd prefer not to go to jail, that's not saying too much. There are other poor substitutes for tolerance. There's the kind that really means you don't give a hoot. Scholars Barrington Moore, Herbert Marcuse, and Paul Wolff called this "pure tolerance" in their book, *A Critique of Pure Tolerance*, and found it indefensible. If you tolerate absolutely everything, you're turning a blind eye to some very ugly things. Would we tolerate heroin addiction, as people of other countries do? Is this tolerance, or is it an abandonment of some of the poorest among us? Would we tolerate child pornography, as people do in some places? Is this tolerance, or is it the abandonment of the powerless among us? Tolerance without compassion is a very cold affair. Then there is the simple I-have-my-opinion-you-have-yours kind of tolerance, which we can call not pure, but passive tolerance. No one's getting hurt. Yet it's not good enough to *say* that others are entitled to their own opinions. If we really mean it, we have to *ensure* that they can have their opinions. We need to promote acceptance. Passive tolerance isn't good enough.

Many of us have seen firsthand the difference between passive tolerance and actual acceptance. A new member enters the family. No one approved of the marriage in the first place. In fact, one aunt didn't send a gift, and a grandfather started mumbling about his will. Two cousins didn't show up for the wedding. At the wedding someone made an unfortunate joke. Others recalled that they had never had real, total confidence in the bride's judgment. Now the groom is no longer a groom, but a full-fledged brother-in-law. He is tolerated. Sometimes he is passively tolerated. That means he's there, but no one's talking to him. He sits on the couch, wanders over to the window, gets a drink, sits on the couch again. Or maybe he is actually accepted. They all dislike him just as much and distrust him even more. They don't believe a word he says, *but they ask him his opinion.*

Acceptance says, "Not only may you enter my world, but you may be yourself in my world. You may enter on your own terms. You may speak. I will ask you to speak. I will defend your right to speak. I will tolerate what you say, even if I detest it, and I will recognize your right to believe—and behave—differently than I do." As Yitzhak Rabin said of his talks with Yasser Arafat, "One doesn't make peace with one's friends." In fact, it can be the mark of a hero to turn an enemy into a friend.

It was the hope of the American founding fathers, of Washington and Jefferson especially, that the old hatreds of Europe would not be transferred to the new nation. That was why America looked so special and so blessed; it was a chance to start over, a place where former enemies could be reconciled as Americans. And often they did become friends. We have a unique two-party political system where alliances and strange bedfellows often ensure election. The political scientist Seymour Martin Lipset described America's political stability as a direct result of these cross-cutting allegiances. No political party, he argued, has people of only one religion or only one social class or only one region. So interests overlap, compromise is crucial and, as a result, enemies can become friends. Sometimes Americans themselves have even seemed less bitter than their foreign cousins, and more willing to make old enemies into useful allies.

Pragmatism is only part of it. Idealism is, in fact, the greater part. Our greatest models are figures who overcame deep hatreds or preached conciliation. The Biblical figure Jacob, haunted by a lifetime of regrets, remembered how he betrayed his father, Isaac, conspired and cooperated with his mother to deceive his father and his brother, Esau, and then spent years running from his brother's anger and vengeance. Jacob's mind was constantly invaded by the memories of his misdeeds, in spite of years spent trying to suppress and forget them. These painful memories were particularly oppressive when Jacob heard that his brother Esau and a company of his men were traveling toward him. Finally, Jacob would have to face both Esau and himself.

Jacob panicked. He sent servants ahead with rich gifts to appease Esau. He divided his camp into two halves, the better to prepare for war. Then he waited.

During that night's sleep beside the Jabbok River, Jacob became as restless as the water. He thought he saw his brother's face in the churning, windblown waters of the Jabbok. He spied the shriveled appearance of his father, Isaac, dancing across the currents. He heard their voices in the cascades. In the chill of the night he had no grand visions of a ladder reaching toward heaven with ascending and descending angels, like his earlier vision of a glorious future.

As Jacob struggled with himself he became agitated, as if locked in battle. His body convulsed; he wept as he struggled. Jacob was ashamed of his past and afraid to meet the future; he wanted to run away once again. But he knew he needed to stand his ground at last, to become someone different from the coward he'd always thought himself to be.

By daybreak Jacob felt transformed. He had made peace with his past and would now refer to himself not as Jacob, from the Hebrew word meaning "heel," but as Israel, a name meaning "he has struggled with God and prevailed." Jacob was calm and slept deeply until the sun was directly overhead. He had not slept so soundly since he was a boy.

He arose and was ready to meet Esau face to face, hoping to change their relationship for the better. He ran toward Esau and embraced him. With tears streaming down his face, he whispered into Esau's ear, "To see your face is like seeing the face of God."

As the brothers journeyed together, reminiscing, Jacob noticed that he now walked with a limp, an injury from his fitful night by the water. "It is not the limp of a battle wound," he told himself. "It is a reminder of my struggle to overcome my past."

Hatred and enmity are the past, friendship the future. Foes become friends, not because they change, but because we change. Jesus, asking men and women to be more perfect, said, "Love your enemies, bless them that curse you, do good to them that hate you, and pray for them which despitefully use you. . . . If you forgive men their trespasses, your heavenly Father will also forgive you: but if you forgive not men their trespasses, neither will your Father forgive your trespasses."

We don't want a holy war in America. Ours is not a tradition of fanaticism, but of forgiveness. The world of hatred is a small, uncreative world.

We are proponents of acceptance, the kind of tolerance that is difficult and requires patient, teeth-gritting effort. We want you to disagree openly, and to agree on what is essential. We propose that religion need not be a divisive element in American public discourse; it need not alienate or exclude. Rather, we invite you to participate in a dialogue. You don't have to give up your identity to speak in America. You don't have to agree on everything. All of us need only recognize that there are others at the table. If we sound a note of advocacy, and prompt you to change your ways, then begin with these principles, above all:

1. Embrace your identity,
2. Engage in dialogue, and
3. Accept the importance of others.

Tolerance is a peculiar characteristic. It is by definition relational. I tolerate you; you tolerate me. There cannot be one tolerant person alone. If politics is the art of compromise, then tolerance is a peculiarly political virtue. It is born of compromise. If one were to ask, "How does a nation become tolerant?" the answer could only be broad and social. Two tolerant people are admirable, a tolerant community is exemplary, but a tolerant nation is created politically, through agreement, cooperation, and compromise.

When we say we are looking for a bigger world, we mean this larger setting where tolerance is the norm. In such a nation, the isolated one would exist only uneasily, out of his or her element, like the skeptic in an age of faith. The bigot would find it hard to defend his or her prejudices by saying, "Some of my best friends . . ." There would be no demons, only women and men of good faith, adversaries struggling to understand one another. In this accepting nation each individual would have worth and each life would have a world of importance. Everyone could experience opportunities for joy, those moments of elation made possible through beauty and freedom and truth. The road would be wide and the journey open to anyone who chooses.

II

Crossing Paths

There is callousness where
there should be caring.

We begin with the story of a forced choice.

Abba Tahnah the Pious walked on the way, struggling to reach the city before sunset. The road was difficult, and, what's more, he was worried about thieves. He carried slung over his shoulder a bundle, and while others might have had bundles either more or less valuable, his was of extreme value to him for it contained his stock-in-trade, his livelihood. There were also a few extra items, something for his wife, and a particular book that had struck his fancy— nothing inappropriate, to be sure, just a book, but it brought him pleasure. He glanced at the sky gauging the hours of light left to travel that day, he looked this way and that, and he examined the road, all the while hurrying as best he could. At a crossroads he came upon a man lying helplessly on the ground. What was wrong with the man? Abba Tahnah looked from the corner of his eye so as not to embarrass the man; all the same, he tried to take in the man's condition. The helpless man was covered with something—boils? lesions? bruises? While Abba Tahnah looked, the man called out, "Master, can you help me? Do an act of kindness for me. Carry me into the city."

Abba Tahnah stopped. He replied, "You see, I carry this heavy bundle. If I put it down in order to carry you, if I abandon it, then how will I support my family? I will forfeit my responsibilities, my household." Abba Tahnah's face fell, and his heart ached as he added quietly, "But to abandon a man in your condition, to turn away, would haunt me. No, it would kill me. I would forfeit my life." He thought for a moment. He tried a tone of strength and resolve. "I do not know how you came to be in that state. And unless you try, I cannot even know the depth of your misery. Stand up and lean on me and perhaps I can help you along and carry my bundle at the same time."

The helpless man sank deeper into the dirt. He didn't explain himself or excuse himself. He didn't beg forgiveness. Dry tears of anguish filled his cheeks, and all he said was, "Please. Do an act of kindness for me."

All at once Abba Tahnah threw his bundle to the ground. Did the man even know how he came to be in that state? And if he knew how, could he ever explain why? Abba Tahnah let his inclination for good overpower his impulse to evil, and he carried the afflicted man into the city. When he returned later to the path to retrieve his bundle, sure enough he found the bundle just as he had left it. Once again he shouldered the pack and hurried toward the city, racing against the sun. Although hours had passed, the sun had barely moved, and it was still light. Abba Tahnah arrived safely in the city just as the first pink clouds hinted at sunset.

Everyone was astonished. The Holy One, Blessed be He, Ruler of the Universe, Creator of Space and Time, had held the sun for Abba Tahnah the Pious, darkness was held at bay, night falling later than it ever had.

৵

WHY ARE SO MANY OF OUR LEGENDS AND LESSONS about the needy? We see it again and again. According to the gospel, when a listener questioned Jesus about the law and the meaning of "Love they neighbor as thyself," Jesus answered with the parable of the good Samaritan. To the question, "Who is my neighbor?" Jesus described a man robbed, beaten, and abandoned. The Samaritan, a stranger to the man, showed compassion and saved him by giving him comfort, care, money, and a place to heal. Jesus did not tell us to greet our neighbor warmly, nor even defer to our neighbor, compliment our neighbor, respect his privacy, or share his meals. Jesus did tell us to care for our fellow human beings. The story of the good Samaritan reminds us that the needy are our neighbors.

One reason the poor and impoverished of spirit figure so

strongly in our history and beliefs is that they have a special relation-ship to God. Jesus was born in a manger, surrounded by straw and mud, as simple as the poorest of peasants. Yet the lack of material wealth allows the spiritual light to shine and goodness to show more brilliantly. Thus was Jesus crowned Prince of Peace in the unlikeliest of castles. The Star of Bethlehem shone most brilliantly in a sky empty of glittering lights. And Jesus taught that the last shall be first, and the first shall be last; that it is easier for a camel to go through the eye of a needle than for a rich man to enter the King-dom of Heaven.

There is more to the special place of the poor than sheer material want. Their suffering on earth reminds us of Jesus' trials on earth. The poor and needy are holy because they deliver God's message. Would a busy commuter, rushing past a homeless beggar, have been too busy to offer Jesus a sip of water on the climb to Calvary? How many Centurions live among us today, making that climb even more painful? Jesus revealed his divinity by healing the afflicted. That act of healing revealed God's good-ness and the hope of redemption. When we reach out to the sick, the poor, and the needy, we embrace God's message of hope and healing.

Those in need are also honored in the Jewish tradition. Jews ask, in a world full of mystery, who knows who that broken traveler really is? If God were to appear as a beggar, how would we treat him? According to Jewish tradition, the prophet Elijah appears as a poor and needy traveler; the fate of mankind hinges on the welcome he receives. So each impoverished soul must be treated as if he were Elijah announcing the coming of the Messiah—for he might be.

How differently would we treat one another if we valued one another differently? A parable tells us just how differently. A small town's two priests and two ministers squabbled bitterly among themselves. There were the usual personality conflicts, the pressures of their work, fatigue. One felt slighted, another unappreciated, a third overworked. One particularly difficult weekend they marched over to the town rabbi's study for an outside opinion. They argued, each trying to present his case.

"Don't you find it disrespectful for large groups to meet in your private offices?"

"I didn't give them permission to meet in your offices; they went in by themselves. . . ."

"But you let them—"

"Don't you people have any dignity?"

"Dignity seems to be in short supply." They turned to the rabbi. "What would you do in such a case?"

The rabbi answered, "I really can't help you. I really can't say anything at all about such a case. But I will say this: as far as my point of view goes, one of you is the Messiah."

After that a new peace came over the town. Not that each clergyman thought he was God, far from it. But each saw the others in an entirely new light. They began to think along these lines: "That selfish, small-minded dogmatist—the Messiah? Perhaps I should treat him more gently. His dogmatism—it's burning passion. His selfishness—it's his sense of mission, isn't it?" We reason differently when we see others as possessing inestimable value and importance.

Each beggar must be treated as a king, for in this world of mystery and madness, he might be. History has taught men and women that the world can be both kind and cruel, and it is sometimes hard to see the scholar through the refugee's rags. The man who is today an outcast may tomorrow be a respected citizen. And then he may be cast out again. So help the needy, and when they are in power they will remember. Or their children will. Or their children's children will.

Finally, there is another reason the poor hold such an important place in our culture and why caring for them is so important to our spiritual lives: When it comes to the life of the spirit, we are all needy. We are all impoverished. No human being is better than any other. We are all in need. On a good day we are all Abba Tahnah the Pious, hurrying along full of strength and nervous energy, lots of worries, lots of responsibilities, some private pleasures, a sense of importance. And full of confidence and faith. But on a bad day we are all helplessly mired on the side of the road. On a bad day the tears of anguish burn our cheeks. We ask why. We say that life is too hard.

Imagine a poor woman one car breakdown away from disaster. If that old car busts a muffler—it's a '78 Ford Galaxy, and it doesn't sound very good—if that car loses its muffler, she's in big trouble. Then she won't be able to get to work, and she'll lose her job. She doesn't have the hundred and fifty dollars to repair it. With no car and no job, she'll have to take her kids to her mother's, because she won't be able to feed them. And her mother is mad. She just hates that new boyfriend and won't let him in her house. Every time the car rumbles and sputters the woman hears her mother lighting into her. The car doesn't sound good, but there's just no choice.

And there we are, rich and poor alike. It doesn't matter if you drive a Galaxy or a Volvo station wagon. You have people depending on you, and it seems impossible to please all of them. You have responsibilities, and the world just won't cooperate. On a good day it all works. On a bad day everyone is lighting into you, and worst of all, you need their help. There's just no choice. It is part of the human condition to be in need. When we see the poor, the sick, and the hungry, we don't just say, There but for the grace of God go I. We say, There is a part of me that looks like that. It may be on the inside, but I, too, understand weakness.

HUMAN CHARACTER:
HUMAN WEAKNESS, HUMAN STRENGTH

Weakness is part of the human condition. It is for that reason that we cannot bestow our acts of help and loving kindness only on those whose behaviors we like or admire. When people become addicted to drugs, they need our help. When people sink in such despair that they cannot work, they need our help. When teenage girls become pregnant, forced into an adult world they can neither handle nor understand, they need our help. How can we deny such people our help when weakness in the face of life's difficulties gnaws at all of us? Jesus said in his Sermon on the Mount,

> Judge not, that ye be not judged. For with what judgment ye judge, ye shall be judged: and with what measure ye mete, it shall be measured to you again. And why beholdest thou the mote that is in thy brother's eye, but considerest not the beam that is in thine own eye? Or how wilt thou say to thy brother, Let me pull out the mote out of thine eye; and, behold, a beam *is* in thine own eye?

In America today a wealthy woman with many choices laid before her may choose to devote her full time, attention, and love to raising her child. Yet when a poor woman decides that devotion to her child is paramount, we call her lazy and irresponsible. So little do we respect caring, we begrudge it even for our children.

Catholic tradition particularly understands weakness as part of the human condition, born of a sin committed by the very first man and woman and present ever since. And if one could preach only to the holy, how many pews would be filled?

When Moses Maimonides, a Jewish philosopher, described acts of charity, he placed high among them charity given anonymously and blindly, where the donor is not named and the recipient is unknown. If the recipient is unknown, his or her behavior is irrelevant. Charity, in this light, comes without strings or qualifications.

Why, in the Gospel according to Saint Matthew, does Jesus advise, let not your left hand know what your right hand does when giving charity? Why should alms be given in secret? Is the message that we should be humble and avoid the trumpets of vainglory? Certainly that is part of it. A boast about one's rectitude blows a trumpet as loud as any other boast, perhaps louder. Yet Jesus' words go beyond right conduct in public; they are about human connection and the meaning of helping others. Just as an individual is of two hands, she is of two minds. She feels generous and expansive in an emotional moment. Then she reconsiders. With one hand she gives. With the other she takes away. But Jesus says that there should be no second thought to giving. When the part of you that cares gives charity, don't even tell the part of you that counts and calculates and reconsiders. When the compassionate, human part gives to others, don't let your dislike of the others or their habits or the part of you that suspects them of no good take hold. Charity should be quiet, but it should be complete. Keep it a secret even from your own doubts. Jesus said, "Give to him that asketh thee and from him that would borrow of thee turn not away." Whoever asks you to go a mile, go with him two.

Why? Because this is the Christian image of God, and human beings strive to be perfect, like God. What Jesus taught was this: of the impulse to harm and the impulse to help, the better one is the impulse to help. But more: the world will make demands on you; people will ask for your help. When they ask, respond. It is not enough to proudly give help to the few whom you deem worthy. The worthy may not ask. It is the one who asks whom you must help.

These are ideals, not policy. Policy should no more parade as ideals than the other way around. If we abandon our ideals, what will appear in their stead? This is our shared wisdom. This is our shared spiritual tradition.

But there is a little bit of policy wisdom we share, gained over thousands of years of religious life: ideals are important, but if you make policy assuming no human frailty, you will fail. People are going to become addicted. They are going to despair. They are going to sin. And what then? Of course we value work. But not everyone can handle a job, some only two days, some only three days a week. What then? Human character is varied, just as human ability is varied. We are rich in a universe of millions of unique temperaments. Rather than punish weakness, let's count our strengths.

What is it that drives women and men forward, allowing them to laugh, to smile, and to keep trying? Our Ford Galaxy owner gets in that car every morning and goes. She doesn't give up. And sure enough, the breakdown happens. She borrows the money for the repair, leaves the kids with her mother, takes the reprimands. And she keeps going. What is that spark that makes people strong?

That spark is caring. The knowledge that we matter makes us strong. Friends make us strong. And some depth of character, some inner light, makes some people stronger than others. We acknowledge that and celebrate it. Strength of character makes heroes of even the poorest and the neediest.

Is it a job that lights that spark and drives people to fulfill their responsibilities and love their neighbors? No. Strong, loving people will shine at work. But it is not the job that sets people's spirits free. How could it be? So many people have jobs only to lead suffocated, selfish lives. If we say well, it's their particular job, then we are dreaming of a world of work that might never exist. Why do some people seek out jobs while others right next to them give up in despair? Or quit? If jobs redeemed men and women, why do some drift in and out of work?

In other words, a minimum-wage, minimum-hope job will not turn around someone's life. It will not force a woman into virtue or a man into dignity. Demanding that the poor do penance at some task is not the same as openly, freely helping them, teaching them. We do not back away from the word *charity*, and we do not back away from the word *entitlement*. We will not demand the punishment of people who are poor, nor the punishment of their children. It is our responsibility to care for them. We do not back away from the word *welfare*, and we do not back away from the word *character*.

Strength of character is the ability to go on in a world that is not perfect. Sometimes that means there are no jobs. Or no fulfilling jobs. Still, one must go on. The world is not perfect, and people are not perfect. Yet the myth of perfection is everywhere, eroding men's and women's spirits. When people believe they must be perfect, they take on too many tasks, fail, and then blame themselves. When people believe the world must be perfect, they despise their fellow human beings, and hatred eats at their hearts. When people do not recognize their own limitations, they do everything poorly and nothing well. Finally, that shimmering, elusive perfection can drive people to alcohol and drugs and abuse of other people all in the hope of escape to something better or more perfect, or to ease the pain of an imperfect world.

Imagine your life as being like a switchboard, the kind receptionists or operators at the telephone company used to use. A few red lights are blinking. One child is having trouble at school, your boss is demanding too much, your neighbor is lodging a complaint about your cable television wires. That is all fine, you can handle it. A few more lights go on: your brother-in-law is out of work, and your parents are pressuring you to take him in. The lights keep going on and blinking. And then one more light goes on—your mother is diagnosed with breast cancer. Everything stops. You are overloaded. Too much is coming in.

The answer is not to become perfect. The answer is not to handle it. The answer is not to build a better switchboard. The answer is to slow down and get help. Maybe you cannot handle it all, but some of the problems and concerns someone else could handle. To insist upon perfection in yourself or someone else is no less than callousness.

In this way, demanding that each individual live alone, self-sufficient—without aid, without health care, without child care—is callous because it is the same as demanding perfection. It is the same as demanding that each person be a butcher, baker, candlestick-maker, computer programmer, travel agent, hunter, fisherman, poet, and critic. For many people that kind of self-sufficiency is an ideal; it just isn't the world we know. So demanding it is impossible and cruel. Here is that poor woman with the miserable car and an even more miserable life. We demand that she find her own job—she is an employment agency. We demand that she find her own care for her child—she is a childcare provider. We demand that she keep her kid away from violence and drugs, at the very same minute that she is traveling an extra few miles to buy her mother's blood-pressure medicine at a cheaper pharmacy. We demand that she create an entire world from scratch. And yet demanding perfection in her is as unfair as demanding it in ourselves.

Look in the mirror. Look honestly at the mote in your eye and the lines around your mouth. How often does your coworker's smile and good morning make the difference between a good day and a bad one? How many times has your friend said, "Oh, forget it, it's not important," and saved you for another day? Now look more deeply. How did it come to pass that you are where you are? Did some distant relative make a choice that would determine your life? Was some ancestor beaten so hard that anyplace other than home looked good? Put aside that American myth of perfection. When we look in the mirror we don't see cowboys. Maybe the rest of the world sees cowboys, but we see people intimately tied to other people, to their history, to the world around them. The idea that Americans succeed alone, each individual alone, is a myth.

Even the most classic of do-it-yourself stories, the stories of the American frontier, are exaggerations and distortions. The "Little House on the Prairie" stories that were serialized on television spun out the myth of the proud, self-suficient, isolated family pitted against the elements of nature, standing or falling on their own efforts without any help from community or government. The stories were so appealing because they were the antithesis of big government. They were so appealing because people long for a simpler life that is purer and more uplifting than the ones they face. According to scholar Stephanie Coontz, the stories were visions of a way of life that never was. The "rugged individuals" who settled the West did it with massive local, territorial, and federal help as well as with the help of friends, neighbors, and communities. It was government land grants, subsidies for building railroads, canals, irrigation projects, and communication networks that allowed the West to flourish.

In America we encourage individual achievement and celebrate individual talents. But without caring there is no achievement. Without nurturing there is no talent. That is the reality of America, not cowboys, not swagger, not cool perfection, not the outlaw and the backwoods trapper. The myth may be self-sufficiency, but the reality has been town meetings, barn raisings, quilting bees, looking out for the neighbor's kids and the community's poor.

The most classic statement about Americans being joiners comes from Alexis de Tocqueville's *Democracy in America*. De Tocqueville was a French visitor who came to the newly formed United States to study the penal system. He was deeply interested in how democratic government is created and sustained, and he wondered what France could learn, for he traveled soon after France's own democratic revolution, but he feared for its future. So he studied not only the government of the new United States, but also the habits of the American people, convinced that the behavior of individuals contributed to a country's government. His observations on the American character have become enduring truths: he saw that without an aristocracy to emulate, Americans simply copied one another and relied on conformity to share their tastes. He remarked that while nearly obsessed with individual well-being, Americans took an avid interest in public affairs, believing that their democratic government would determine their fate in the world. He was optimistic about American industry and deeply critical of slavery. Above all, he remarked that American democracy was actually upheld by the American tendency to join together in voluntary association.

Americans, he noted, were fond of mutual aid societies. They had innumerable self-governing clubs, agencies, interest groups, a kind of "tumult." He wrote,

> No sooner do you set foot upon American ground, than you are stunned by a kind of tumult; a confused clamor is heard on every side; and a thousand simultaneous voices demand the satisfaction of their social wants. Everything is in motion around you; here, the people of one quarter of a town are met to decide upon the building of a church; . . . in another place, the laborers of a village quit their ploughs to deliberate upon the project of a road or a public school.

All of this activity accomplished several ends. According to de Tocqueville, it gave Americans practice in democratic government; it created an optimism, an American can-do feeling, that social confidence that lets citizens trust other citizens. The right to associate freely made Americans distinctive and distinctively social.

Social. As early as 1831 de Tocqueville saw the country as distinctively social, as a place where people depended upon one another for everything from superficial style to the most fundamental justice. He saw America as lacking in individual greatness, but full of cooperation, a place where "the great bond of humanity is strengthened."

Now, over one hundred and sixty years after de Tocqueville, Americans' view of ourselves is uncertain. For some reason the barn raisings and irrigation projects are not as prominent in our minds as bootstraps and cowboys. Have we succumbed to Westerns, sit-coms, and advertising? The mutual aid societies have faded next to tales of millionaires. Who are we really in this amazing experiment of a country? How do we care for one another?

AMERICA AND ITS INSTITUTIONS

An institution is an organized way people have of caring for one another. It lasts more than a generation. Sometimes there is a building, like a post office. But sometimes there is no building. We call the family an institution, yet it has no headquarters, flies no flag, and doesn't even have a motto. From one generation to the next people take on the jobs of family life—father, mother, children, grandparents. There have been bad institutions. Slavery was an American institution of ugly, evil dimensions. When some people speak of institutionalized racism in this country, they mean that racial discrimination has become an answer, a way of making decisions, making choices, framing questions. But not all institutions are bad. Every once in a while the local post office finds a check lost in the mail fifty years before and delivers it to some surprised and slightly ruffled grandson of the original addressee. You can be sure he is glad it is the same postal system now as it was in his grandmother's time. Needless to say, religious institutions such as the Episcopal Church, the Catholic Church, and Jewish synagogues and philanthropies are structures people have used to care for one another for a long time. Sometimes the word *institution* disguises the original purpose, which was for people to work together.

Institutions are big. They are bigger than one person and last for more than one generation. So their language can sound stilted, outdated, or actually laughable. We laugh at legalese, and we strain at forms and questionnaires; we label them bureaucratese. Perhaps years ago the words made more sense. In some American families today the children still call their parents Mother and Father. But in many other families that traditional language sounds stilted and formal. Sometimes the language of tradition is uplifting; sometimes it presents an obstacle to understanding. And people disagree on this. Jews disagree on how much of the worship service should be in Hebrew. There are synagogues whose services are totally in Hebrew; others hold services that have very little. Some Catholics still like to hear a Mass in Latin, but for others Latin only muffles the message. Episcopalians have differences of opinion about what versions of the church service they approve of—some like the service based on the 1928 Book of Common Prayer; others like the Rite II, which has more modern and simplified language. Institutions change and must change if they are to speak to people of new generations living under new conditions.

American religious institutions still care. But for many Americans the big heavy doors have become too big, and the burden of opening those doors has become great. Some people say it is just that Americans are out of practice. Or that American life simply doesn't respect religious belief and doesn't encourage people to seek answers in church. But there is also a movement to make places of worship more welcoming, better able to speak to Americans today. For institutions, with all their weighty and timebound ways, with all their size and formality, are tough, resilient things. They last. They work over and over again. They do a job. Alexis de Tocqueville described one of religion's jobs when he recounted how religion in America kept individuals from focusing exclusively on themselves and how it worked in a democracy as a strong social glue. His observations on the important place of religion in America seem very true today, when the United States is one of the most religious nations in the world. On every measure such as church attendance and belief in God, Americans register strong devotion and satisfaction with religion's place in America.

America's religious institutions have done a very good job at caring for the poor and needy. Here in America we have done a good job taking care of our poor. Consider the job of America's religious institutions, historically and today. Between 1890 and 1920 millions of refugees arrived in America with nothing but the strength of their will and often even that was broken. They did not speak English. Some of them did not come from countries with democratic traditions. And they were poor. There is a pleasant myth among some of these immigrants' snootier grandchildren that they made it alone. Each tough little newcomer was a Horatio Alger newsboy, as this story has it. He saved, invested, married a resourceful and economical wife, and founded a dynasty. Or better yet, he studied. He studied nights while selling tremendously clever widgets days, or while working in a sweatshop. Every family knows of a ditch digger who became a successful contractor or a woman with one or two boarders who bought several apartment buildings.

Let us look at the real America. Even the cowboys didn't do it alone. Where there wasn't the family, there was the village association. Where there wasn't the village association, there was the union. Where there wasn't the union, there was the neighborhood or the parish. Even the settlement patterns of the newcomers attest to their need for help and their desire for a caring community. The poor in nineteenth-century Italy worked at the whim of landowners who sent them to work in distant fields, imposing a backbreaking loneliness. The freedom of America allowed these people to live as families around the corner from the factory, which was all many immigrants had dreamed. Where could one buy food? And for all those so-called self-made men, to whom could one sell food? The neighborhood. And behind it all, everywhere, there were Christian and Jewish philanthropies looking out for the indigent, lost, and homeless.

Religious institutions educated poor children for minimal cost or even for free. They supported widows and orphans, gave loans to small businessmen, all the while encouraging philanthropy among the privileged. Moreover, they provided the social services and ac-culturation services crucial to dislocated and impoverished newcom-ers—they counseled the suicidal, disciplined violent youth, encouraged the gifted, and gave communities focus and coherence. There is a story about a young, very Americanized man, a free thinker, who chided his father, also a free thinker and an atheist, for continuing to attend Sabbath services every Friday night. "You don't believe a word of it," the son laughed. "Why do you go?"

"Well," the father said, "Ginsburg goes. So Ginsburg goes to talk to God, and I go to talk to Ginsburg."

Many of the immigrants during the early years of this century actually came to escape tradition's heavy hand. As free thinkers and socialists they didn't care much for religion and religious practice. Yet even they recognized the power and significance of these caring institutions. In some groups Catholic men left church attendance to their wives, who were responsible for the family's spiritual lives. The Church was part of their lives, if not directly, then indirectly. An avowed Jewish Socialist wrote to *The Daily Forward*'s letters column ("The Bintel Brief," the Dear Abby of the Yiddish press) that although he certainly would not attend High Holy Day services, he felt awkward picketing or otherwise disturbing the service. *The Forward*, a Yiddish, Socialist newspaper, answered, in effect, do what you feel, but do not interrupt services. In other words, no matter what the politics or even the theology of these new Americans, they respected the power of the caring institutions that went far beyond them in time, in magnitude, and in their ability to help people.

One young boy on New York's Lower East Side was particularly tough and very brash. He had grown up without a father. His mother had struggled in the needle trades. He had spent his early years in and out of Jewish day orphanages and drifted through Hebrew schools until he could get some work pushing racks in the garment district. He became active in the union. A few weeks before his thirteenth birthday he burst into the rabbi's office and announced, "I am not becoming bar mitzvah. I am a Socialist." The rabbi, old, wise, a little sarcastic, also a disciplinarian, looked up with a wry smile on his lips. "Do you think God cares?" he said.

Even the nonbeliever had to engage in a dialogue with the synagogue, the church; even an atheist had to declare his intentions to God. And as for God, the petty affairs of a thirteen-year-old's political beliefs were beside the point. And as for the religious institutions, the particular strengths and weaknesses of their congregants or communities were beside the point. The point was keeping people whole. The point was keeping people engaged in the dialogue.

Religious institutions have done that job in the past. Some may have given up the responsibility, but many are still on the front lines today, fighting poverty, illiteracy, and homelessness. The

Episcopal Church runs shelters, recovery programs, food programs, job training programs, counseling, every social service that people need. They do it for today's needy: inner-city youth, the homeless, the hungry, today's newcomers. If a poor woman and her family arrive at one of the shelters, they get medical attention, meals, counseling, and a safe place to stay. They get these things not because they are Episcopalians or engage in prescribed behavior or even because they are begging. They get these things because they need them and to turn them away would be unconscionable. And Catholic Charities, the largest private provider of AIDS/HIV care in San Francisco, does the same, and Jewish Services does the same.

THE GOVERNMENT AS A CARING INSTITUTION

Every Western industrialized democracy has some provision for caring for the poor. One reason for this is political. Democracies lose stability when a large poor underclass feels alienated and without hope. The fear of political instability led to many of the depression-era reforms and prompted George Marshall to develop his plan for aid to postwar Europe. Helping the poor proved good democratic policy in both the United States and Europe. Another reason is economic. The Western industrialized countries are wealthy countries. Over centuries many have accumulated wealth from the resources of their colonies and the growth of industry. As a result they are able to afford to provide a better life for their citizens. As one social scientist said when writing about providing housing, "We should do it because we CAN do it." This was one driving idea behind Lyndon Johnson's Great Society and his War on Poverty of the 1960s. In a truly Great Society, he argued, could children go hungry and disease go untreated? Poverty in the midst of great wealth seemed an ugly and embarrassing blight, a horrible gash on an otherwise perfect countenance. There are also historical reasons why Western democracies have been concerned about their needy, reasons having to do with increased understanding of human biology, psychology, criminology, and technological advances in medicine, agriculture, and construction.

But we would like to think that there is another reason that Western industrialized democracies have cared for their poor. These countries share a common heritage, a common set of values stemming from their religious roots. Their values live in the minds and hearts of their citizens, voters, policy makers, judges, and critics. There need not be one official religion in America, nor one official religious observance. There is an American tradition strong enough to embrace everyone. We need not shout our beliefs from the rooftops. We live them, vote them, and act on them every day.

Right now in America there is a movement away from the government as a caring institution. Now more and more people are crying more and more loudly to reinvent the wheel. The louder they cry, the more it sounds as if they don't like wheels and want to get rid of them altogether. There is also a movement away from caring. Callousness has become the order of the day. The lack of faith in government and the lack of faith in fellow human beings are related. People are afraid that the great American experiment is failing: that the underclass cannot be wished away with depression-era reforms, that America is not wealthy enough to help, and that history has not always been kind with its so-called advances and morally ambiguous technology. People reason to themselves, if I feel alone, pressured, and weak, how can I help you? People feel the forced choice, the tension between self-sacrifice and helping the needy. What if there isn't a happy ending? What if we are drawn in beyond our ability? What if we lose everything? We all sound like Abba Tahnah, worrying about his bundle and his obligations. "If I stop to help you, I will lose everything I have," Abba Tahnah thought. And Americans are now at that same crossroads, feeling that same uncertainty.

So the United States government is going to leave the business of caring, not because it cannot do it. Not because it cannot distribute free vaccines or provide jobs or job training or housing. Because it will not do it. And that is reason enough, after all. Government is no more than an institution, and an institution is no more than people working together to do a job. And many Americans do not want their government to do that job. We understand that. Government is big, so its workers cannot always respond quickly. Washington can seem distant, and of late the federal government has felt the squeeze on resources.

At the same time we will not condone the drain of values from American public life. The American government must not leave behind its roots in caring and providing for the poor. If the United States were to leave it behind altogether, it would signal an abandonment of some of Western society's highest ideals. When the people of the United States state unequivocally in law that they care nothing for those who cannot help themselves, that will be the true decivilization of America. When they tell the weakest of God's creatures, "Go hang," that will be the true age of darkness. The physical suffering will be enormous. But the moral suffering will be irreparable.

If religious institutions were run for profit, the course would be clear. The largest competitor in the welfare industry, government, would quit the field declaring it unprofitable. It's an impossible task, they would say. Well, the profit-seeking church would get out, too, just the way companies got out of the backyard pump business or horse and buggy manufacture. One company sees the writing on the wall first, and eventually all the companies understand it is no longer a profitable line. But churches are not for-profit institutions. They cannot abandon ideas and ideals with the whim of a market. Religious charities and philanthropies will exist whether or not the American voters vote to help the poor. The question is, who will help?

Initiatives to decentralize government programs by giving block grants to the states to administer social programs will not work. State and local governments have abysmal track records. They simply do not care for the needy, have not done it in the past, and, as state governors themselves have worried aloud, they do not have the machinery in place to do it in the future. That would truly be reinventing the wheel only to get rid of wheels altogether. Look again at the real America. Someone is actually providing meals for the indigent. Is it the Salvation Army, Saint Anthony's Soup Kitchen, the San Francisco Food Bank? Thousands of organizations scrape by on miniscule operating budgets, begged from local residents. Is it Jewish Services for the Aged, the Episcopal Sanctuary, Meals on Wheels? Imagine if money went where it actually helped, imagine how many more people could be fed, housed, clothed, and treated. Imagine a safety net of such fine weave that if there were a single person begging on a street corner, he would be found and comforted before a second could appear.

We do not want the American people to abandon their concern for the poor, and we do not want the federal government to abandon its efforts. What we do want is a partnership. No single institution, religious or secular, can re-create the federal government's ability to coordinate and to mobilize both people and money. But that doesn't mean that the federal government is the best organization to run a soup kitchen or decide when an indigent man's toenails must be trimmed. No single institution can ensure equal treatment and equal accessibility as well as the federal government. But that doesn't mean that every indigent woman must sleep in a bed owned and purchased by the government. We are calling for a partnership, a triangle of care with three points: religious charities, government, and community. We want the federal government's support and coordination. We need a government clearing house, a government granting office, a government quality commission. We need a government that openly expresses its desire to make this country a better place for both rich and poor. We want the community's backing and help. We need private industries with public consciences and community groups that will step in to help us weather change, financial and political. We will bring to the partnership our know-how, our experience, and our intense commitment.

ABBA TAHNAH THE PIOUS STOOPED TO LIFT THE MAN *at the crossroads. The man gave off a foul smell. Abba Tahnah carried him in his arms, as quickly as he could. What happened to this man? he wondered. How did his fingernails become so bloody and black? Why did he need to get to the city? Did he know someone there who would care for him? If he did, did that person know he was coming? Why did his family let him suffer this way? Abba Tahnah let his thoughts run in these directions, but he asked the man no questions for fear that he would increase the man's anguish. Abba Tahnah's foot hit a stone, and as his weight shifted awkwardly a pain burst into his side. He thought, Dear God, was it something I did that hurt this man? Is that why you put him in my path? But I didn't know him. Did I? Abba Tahnah tried to decipher the man's features. As he looked more and more closely, he saw less and less until all he saw was the center of the man's eye. And then the strangest thing happened. While Abba Tahnah looked into the man's eye, time stopped. Abba Tahnah couldn't hear anything or see anything. Even the foul smell was gone. He was consumed by this eye, the center of which was the sun, still high in the sky. He saw the sun in the man's eye. That was when he knew that he had done the right thing, that he had done what God intended. Abba Tahnah's strength doubled and his pace quickened.*

IN OUR SHARED TRADITION IT IS IMMORAL TO LET children starve because their parents are poor or black or addicted to drugs. It is immoral to turn away and say that if they're tough they'll survive. And it is immoral to say that some must starve now so that others later can live, or that they will be the "costs" of a "system," for God turned Abraham away from human sacrifice.

This value on helping others goes by many names. We call it *karitas* or *tzdakah*, charity or philanthropy; we call it caring, decency, brotherly love; we call it *menschlichkeit* or human kindness, compassion, loving kindness. We call it humanity, and it is one of our proudest traditions.

III

Crossing Rivers

There is isolation where there should be community.

A bishop embraces solidarity.

THE DELAWARE RIVER

In 1789 Samuel Seabury faced a desperate and depressing scene. The American colonists had won their independence, and, as he had feared, not only good had come of it. As a man of conscience and a clergyman he had tried to warn them. He had spoken out against the violence, the riots, the tarring and feathering, hanging and burning by street mobs and fanatics. Then there was the war. He had done his best to minister to the troops, young boys, scared; they were so far from home. And fighting for what? Under the red coats they were children of God and someone's sons, dying in such a wild place. Well, the fighting finally ended, and a new country was begun. So apparently there was some hope for some kind of law on this continent. But the Church. His beloved Church of England. His prediction was right, only it was the Church, not the courts, that was being gnawed to death by rats and vermin.

It was not a religious age; he understood that. People wanted political answers or even scientific answers. Church membership was low everywhere. And even those who did belong to the Anglican Church had favored revolution and independence over church loyalty. Most of the signers of the Declaration of Independence had been Anglicans. Even the Anglican clergy in many places had been overwhelmingly on the side of the colonists against England. But the war had made everything worse for the Church. So many clergymen had fled. So many people had forsaken so much of their past. In just a few short years the Anglican Church in America had gone from an official religion to a despised and hunted minority. No more than a handful of ministers had met and chosen him to seek consecration as a bishop. Seabury had failed in England and had only become America's first Anglican bishop after consecration in Scotland in 1784.

So there he was, bishop of an empty church. The only two other bishops, consecrated by England were known revolutionaries who curried favor with the laity. Now Massachusetts wanted him to join the other two bishops in consecrating another bishop. Could he join with them? They would ruin the Church. Their religious ideas bordered on sacrilege, and their political ideas repulsed him. If he stood his ground, however, he would stand alone. Alone his doctrine was pure. Joined with theirs it was muddy. Alone his conscience was clean. Joined with them he had to justify unholy compromises. Alone his powers was strong. If he joined with the bishops, the laity grasped power. But alone he had no church.

Bishop Seabury did join the others in the convention of 1789, did compromise, and in so doing created the Protestant Episcopal Church of the United States. Community was worth the compromise, even at the cost of losing power, even at the cost of losing certainty.

℘

THE PAST, ESPECIALLY THE AMERICAN REVOLUTIONARY past, always looks so blessed with certainty. Founding Fathers stare out forthrightly from posed portraits. The strain of doubt is smoothed over in brushstrokes, and the poses imply composure. There is the famous portrait of George Washington crossing the Delaware, and he is standing, confidently, gazing into the future. Well, he was crossing into the future, that is true. He probably knew that. He was founding a new country. But just as no one can stand erect in a boat on a rocky and dangerous sea, no human heart can make judgments free of ambivalence and ambiguity. The ambiguity of the human heart afflicts us, as it did the figures of long ago. What is more, there are recurring doubts and ambiguities, questions that plague us whether we are Founding Fathers or simple citizens, whether we are planning a new nation or just trying to makes ends meet. When you think of the Delaware River, think of that rocky sea that leads to a new nation. Think of the attempt at certainty in uncertain times.

These are uncertain times. Like Bishop Seabury, we are seeking a community, but we struggle with the dilemma: alone or together? Being alone is not altogether a bad thing. Peace, reflection, concentration, these are solitary virtues. Similarly, when a group withdraws from other groups it can pursue unity of purpose, it can maintain traditions, and it can foster peace. Yet, as difficult as it may be to forgo these blessings, we choose community. The human heart approaches, retreats, approaches, and retreats from the stranger, from those different in appearance, aspect, or belief. But in our shared tradition, community is such an important value that again and again we try to overcome our fears. Like Samuel Seabury, we choose community. Like Samuel Seabury, we think that the future lies in community.

It isn't only certainty we read into the old portraits; it is also sameness. Somehow when we look back in time, we don't see the shock and terror and differences of the age. The people we call Anglo-Saxons were, hundreds of years ago, Saxon-Normans. The Norman oppression of the Saxons was brutal, total, and unforgiving. Now there's no difference between the two peoples; we barely think of it. Imagine Bishop Seabury's shock and horror at collaborating with patriots, people who would kill their own English cousins and leap like crazed men and women into an unknown world. Today Loyalists and Patriots look alike to us; time seems to have made them more similar.

There was, very recently, an Episcopal clergyman who returned to visit the South, where he was born. He attended a service and smiled when he heard that the Citadel Marching Band would grace the occasion. Then he reflected on the sad history of the Citadel, a military school whose origins lay in the South of slavery and bigotry. Wasn't it used as a military outpost to ensure white power in a place where black slaves outnumbered white slaveowners? Lost in these thoughts, he looked up to the sounds of music and saw that the band was mostly black. Of all those in the room, of course, only he registered surprise. What would have been unthinkable a hundred and fifty years before had become absolutely unremarkable. Buoyed by this observation he said to a cadet, "Soon there'll be lots of women in the band."

"Women? Never." The cadet was outraged. But don't you know what happens next in this story? Can't you see that what looks impossible today will be very possible in years to come? We move further and further toward inclusion, toward community.

This is one reason we feel community is our future—it's just a fact of life. Catholics live all over the world; Jews live all over the world; Anglicans live all over the world. We are already inclusive and varied in our makeup; how can we love anything else? Whether it was peace or war, domination or persecution that brought us to this point, we share this lesson in common: inclusion is powerful and inevitable. When Catholics embrace Our Lady of Guadaloupe, a saint of dark complexion, when Anglicans understand that a majority of Anglican bishops are people of color, when Jews learn new languages just to speak with one another, we see that the value placed on community has already given us the strength to overcome differences and cross rivers.

At the same time, this is not enough. The simple, practical statement "That's who we are" is not enough to explain our desire to welcome people different from ourselves. It's hard to be with people different from ourselves. Why can't community just mean helping the people in your town? Why do we have to use this value on community to support affirmative action or support immigration?

What does it mean to say that community is our destiny? The answer to that question is not a simple fact of life; it is an act of belief. Community is not just about who we are; it is about who we will become.

A parable from the Jewish legends of Midrash tells of heaven and hell. God grants one man a chance to peer into the beyond, to understand the difference between the reward of the righteous and the punishment of the wicked. He sees in hell a banquet table laid for a feast. It is magnificent. Every delicacy is there, but also every staple, every food that people crave and others they dream of tasting at least once. The aroma is warm, spicy, and familiar all at once. Around the table there are diners. All the chairs are full. The diners are all starving. They cannot touch a morsel. For their elbows are fused so that they cannot bend their arms to reach food and bring it to their mouths. They are unable to eat.

In heaven the man is shocked to see the same banquet table. The same food. The same aroma. The same diners. And unbelievably, the diners have the same strange arms with the fused elbows. Yet here all the people are fat and happy, enjoying a feast beyond any in this world, and they are satisfied in a way people on earth do not experience. What explains this difference? In heaven the people feed one another.

If there is a Final Judgment and a world hereafter, if there is a Kingdom of Heaven and a Day of Rejoicing, if there is an end to our burdens, an end to death and sorrow and crying, and if there is a Holy City, then all the nations will be bid to enter. And at that time we will not have our earthly disguises, and we will be joined, all souls together, in the glory of the New Jerusalem. We will be called to join together in a community of angels. Any small and faltering steps we take here on earth to learn about living together are the first lessons toward this greater glory.

The early Protestants of the American colonies believed these words. They thought of their new country as the New Jerusalem, as a chance to try, yet again, to establish God's Kingdom on Earth. And we, we are still in kindergarten, in nursery school, compared to what we need to know to create that holy community of souls living together. We are still trying.

This is not calculation; it is belief. At the root of our most cherished values are beliefs about who we are and what we are trying to do. We believe that the just and virtuous will be rewarded; we believe that how we spend our time here matters. We are here to learn, to accomplish something, to try. We're not sure why, but we know that the choices we make matter.

Community is our destiny in this experimental democracy, America, and in our greater purpose on earth. The more we live together, the more we understand one another. The more we understand one another, the more we accomplish our human purpose. We embrace our life together because community can accomplish great things. It has accomplished great things. It created a country. It built a country.

THE RIVER JORDAN

Two great movements of people between 1864 and 1964 changed the face of the United States. One was the great migration of African-Americans from the rural South to the urban North, and the other was the great wave of European immigrants to American shores. Whether you think of the Mighty Jordan as the Ohio River, which brought slaves and then former slaves out of the South, or as the Atlantic Ocean which brought Eastern Europeans west, think of the River Jordan as that passage to the Promised Land, to that better place. The rocky sea of the Delaware was doubt. When you cross the Jordan you tremble from tyranny and oppression. Men and women crossed it in order to participate as equals in a free society.

Today the growing division between the powerful and the powerless in this country threatens our community. The words sound grand. Powerful. Most of us, even the most comfortably well off, don't feel powerful. What does power mean in this complicated country where people rush to buy guns not because they feel strong, but because they feel weak? Even celebrities demur and point to one another in envy or in tribute. Power used to mean an army and a laurel wreath. Now power is no more than the ability to control the conditions of one's own life. No more and no less.

America is dividing, slowly and steadily, into two societies, one able to control the conditions of its life and the other subject to chance, disaster, and misfortune. Those in the first group, the powerful, have all kinds of choices open to them. If they don't like their jobs they can quit and find others. They can visit doctors regularly. They can move far away, independent of family help. They can save for retirement, send their children to college, own a home. They can move again. They can find mates easily. Their lives are cushioned with quiet and privacy. For them nature is benign—the air is clean, and after an earthquake they can rebuild.

America's second society is very different. These people work hard, they have jobs, just like the first group. But for them it's not easy to find a different job. They might worry about losing their insurance. They might not have insurance at all. Their babies may not go for well-baby checkups because their insurance doesn't cover it. If an adult falls ill, the family might lose the house. They might not have a house. Independence from family is a luxury undreamed of. Young adults might still live with their parents to save on rent. The grind of work, the lack of privacy, the inability to move around makes finding companionship difficult. A flood might destroy a promising child's chance at school by eating up the family's small savings.

What's the difference between these two societies? Is it money? Partly. America is becoming a land of haves and have-nots. Is it race? Partly. Members of minority groups have a harder time in this country. Is it gender? Partly. Women and children make up the largest percentage of the impoverished. Is it education? Yes, but above all it is the way education is used. According to Robert Reich, former secretary of labor and an expert on American industry, the difference between power and powerlessness in our country is related to one's position in the global economy. America's first society, its powerful group, is safe from changes in the local economy. But America's second society is dependent only on the local economy. That means that when construction is in a slump, there is a carpenter whose family cannot see a doctor. He falls ill and turns to the American government. That carpenter is frustrated and furious, because he can't control the conditions of his own life. He's powerless.

This divide between the powerful and the powerless threatens the American sense of community. Members of a highly educated elite that moves at will and develops no connections to the local carpenter, teacher, and grocery check-out clerk risk losing their sense of community responsibility. Those who belong to a poorly educated lower class that is paralyzed in its movement and provincial in its outlook risk losing their sense of hope. The issue here is not compassion, just as it's not moral failure, human frailty, or loving kindness. We are talking about community, pure and simple. Are we in America all in the same boat or are we not? How can we work together to cross this divide and make a stronger, better country, one in which we enjoy both local connection and global competitiveness?

Our shared religious tradition values community. That means that the software engineer who works for a Japanese firm can live alongside the dishwasher repairman who is in business for himself. They can pool their choices, share their resources, and help build a stronger country. Two societies, powerful and powerless, are not half as good as the other American model: one society, free and equal. All three of our religious histories embody a sense of local responsibility and community involvement that goes far beyond the heyday of "community center" religious buildings in the 1960s and 1970s. The ethic of giving back to the community has made Episcopalian, Jewish, and especially Catholic mayors prominent American political figures.

In fact, the Catholic concern over the divide between powerful and powerless has deep historical roots. Long before Franklin Roosevelt's New Deal, Catholic observers of American society expressed concern over the dangerous, difficult, and precarious life of the American worker. Dorothy Day in her publication *The Catholic Worker* was a prominent voice for labor reform in the 1920s. Ideas common to the Catholic movement for justice were later incorporated in New Deal solutions: social security, the eight-hour workday, the just wage. There is a long tradition of American Catholic bishops speaking out on behalf of the powerless and disenfranchised. In St. Louis and New York the Catholic clergy have fought for desegregation.

Compassion is certainly one element of Catholicism, but there is also a very specific Catholic message about community in this tradition of social concern. Catholicism is a religion based on tradition and discipline, both of which are intended to serve as moral rudders. For centuries Catholic discipline has taught the powerful to view their power with perspective and humility. Great European aristocrats built cathedrals to keep their people together and monasteries for study and prayer, remembering Jesus' words that they should give to Caesar what is Caesar's and give to God that which is God's. Many aristocrats chose to give up Caesar's world of power altogether and retire to religious communities as private, pious souls.

The catechism of the Catholic Church actually defines

human life as life in society; there is no fully human life without community. The human person needs to live in society. In Boston's North End, the traditionally Italian part of the city, widows showed such remarkable resilience and ability to cope with their grief that in the late 1970s a young Catholic researcher asked to talk with them. This researcher, Michelle DiPaolo, found some interesting facts about the lives of these women, but especially about their life in the community. The truth was that for many of these women widowhood had brought a respect and authority they had never before enjoyed. Some had become the head of their household. Some had simply acquired an age and experience that commanded respect. Many had been married to men much older than them-selves, and, paradoxically, widowhood made them young again—they could walk farther and faster than they had for a long time. What they had in common was the appearance of traditional Italian widows; their head-to-toe black clothes marked them as members of a distinct group. And it turns out that this group identity, this communal association, was their greatest help in their time of grief. Did any consider putting away the black and living as "private citizens"? Some, but not many. Their neighborhood's respect for them helped them absorb a painful personal loss.

Almost twenty years have passed since that research, and it is now common to hear about support groups and grieving groups. It is now common knowledge that women who suffer a loss often fare better than their male counterparts, because women, in the course of their lives, are more often encouraged to seek social con-tact.

Catholicism's idea of community goes beyond achieving indi-vidual needs. It carries a particular message of service to others. It is not a whim, but a duty to be a neighbor to others, especially the disadvantaged. The common good is a tenet of Catholic faith. One reason the Catholic Church can be unequivocal in its description of human life as community life is that as abstract as *community* sounds, it serves to describe all kinds of groupings made up of unique individuals, each single one recognized as important. The kindergarten teacher who serves her community actually sees twenty-five special little people, each one a fascinating, amazing creation. The hospice nurse who helps the terminally ill sees his job as comforting individual human beings in need of human kindness. Social service is service to the human person. And so the word or idea *community* is not abstract at all; it is a natural part of people's lives.

With this ethic of service and dedication to the common good, Catholic families have produced nurses, lawyers, teachers, priests and nuns, political figures, and medical research doctors. Now there is an established class of American Catholics with wealth and position and, yes, considerable power. Many American Catholics belong to that first society of the highly educated global class. Now the Catholic message of inclusion and concern for the disenfranchised, the Catholic message of community can speak with authority. Catholics in America are a large group; they represent the single wealthiest group in the country and the most educated minority, in absolute terms. When Catholics speak of community, America will listen. When they speak of inclusion, America will listen. When they say, "Train our children so that no American is left behind, powerless," America will listen. When they say, "Give every worker a just wage and fair representation," America will listen. These are the Catholic values of decency, community, and equality.

Almost no part of America today, including American religion, can be understood without thinking about the great migrations, the escape from tyranny, and the drive toward equality. These episodes define who we are and how we live. Our cities, our laws, our work and our play, our movies, music, scholarship, and science all come out of our particular blend of peoples. Our attempts at community must be viewed in the light of race and immigration. Have we forged a community? Have we recognized one another as partners and companions?

Yes and no. If African-Americans had not found jobs in Detroit's auto industry or in the defense industry in California and Italians and Russian Jews had not found jobs in New York's garment industry, this would be a very different country. Community worked when it came to building a strong economy, fighting overseas, and making the GI Bill the backbone of a strong middle class. But still there is isolation where there should be community. That isolation has a name: racism.

Racism is an apartheid of the heart. It is separating oneself from whole parts of humanity and denying individuals their human individuality. No law can change people's inner feelings, we understand that. No government can tell men and women whom to like or dislike. But who will speak of the human heart? Who will speak of the human spirit? Who will help Americans be their best selves rather than their worst selves? It is to the American spirit that we speak when we say that following our shared tradition, affirmative action is morally right. The effort to compensate for the continuing effects of racism—and sexism—is part of listening to our better selves. It is a good way, a moral way, to work toward community.

Now, morality is not policy. Within each of our communities there are reservations about the course of public policy. Jews are sensitive about the idea of quotas, because quotas were used against Jews in the past as a weapon, not an aid. Episcopalians would argue for a more flexible approach to policy, where individual programs or cases could be considered on their merits. Many Catholics are concerned about the economic future and the fair distribution of jobs. Yet despite these policy reservations, we can say that morally affirmative action is part of who we are.

Affirmative action is part of America as that New Jerusalem, that dream of the Protestant colonists who vowed to make this country better, more just, more decent than other countries, and closer to God's will. They meant that they would strive to make it that better place. They meant that this new country was an opportunity to do better. Just as abolitionism had Protestant roots, Protestants today continue to work toward that more decent America. Affirmative action is also part of Catholics' social action and their belief in the fundamental equality of all human beings. And Jewish tradition has a very specific legacy to describe the moral aspect of affirmative action. There are deeply rooted religious and cultural reasons why Jews are committed to civil rights, which go beyond self-interest or 60s nostalgia. Most Jews in America consider an interest in social justice an intrinsic part of their Jewish identity. Such work is a continuation of God's work. Injustices on earth are not God's failing, in the Jewish view, but humanity's assignment. For a Jew, searching for the life of holiness is about finding ways to build a better world—and a just and compassionate society.

There was a rabbi, Moshe Lieb, who believed that every impulse—good or bad—could be put to the service of God. As the rabbi spoke, he began to wonder about the impulse to deny the very existence of God. "How," he wondered, "could the denial of God become a way of serving God? Even disbelief must have some purpose," he thought, "or God would not have created it." He thought about this, and when he realized that even this impulse could be put to good use, he taught: "If someone comes to you and asks for your help, you must not say to him, 'Have faith; God will help you.' You must act as if there were no God, as if help could come only from you, and then you must take the place of God, as it were, and act with loving kindness." The Reform prayer book says something similar: "Pray as if everything depends on God; act as if everything depends on you."

It is up to us to repair the world and make it a better place. In the Jewish view, God and His creations are partners; and the work is not always evenly divided. Once there was a farmer, who struggled and worked like any farmer. A passerby approached his farm and marveled at the order of the fields, how green and prosperous it all looked, and how fertile. The passerby commented to the farmer, "How wonderful to see the fruits of man's work in partnership with God." The farmer sniffed. "Some partnership. You should have seen this place when only God was managing it."

The main task of this partnership, of course, is to find justice. Justice is so close to the Jewish meaning of life that one of Judaism's greatest heroes is King Solomon, a wise judge. He was a great judge not only of what was right, but also of human character. The stories of Solomon's decisions are many. Perhaps the most famous decision is in the case of two women, each of whom demanded custody of an infant as his rightful mother. Solomon knew that if he declared the fair solution to be sharing the baby by cutting it in half, the real mother would recoil and retract her claim.

Justice is so important that Judaism's fools are foolish for their bad judgments and silly conclusions. Those most foolish of all fools, the fictional Wise Men of Chelm, distort justice time and time again, like the time they had to punish a stupid carp.

As Isaac Bashevis Singer tells it, a fish, an ordinary Friday-night destined-to-to-be-chopped-and-cooked fish, had the audacity to lift its tail and slap the town's elder statesman. Punishment was due, surely. But what punishment should be meted out to a creature whose fellows were routinely killed and cooked? Something special. While the elders pondered, the fish swam in a special tank.

"Can a fish be hanged? It has no neck."

"It must have a punishment no fish has ever had before."

"That is difficult. Almost everything has been done to fish."

The Wise Men of Chelm reflected for six months, at the end of which time the village elder reached his verdict: "It must be drowned." They threw the fish in the lake. Now there is justice. So thought the fools.

Along with justice there is law. From the Ten Commandments to the thousands of pages of the Talmud (the treatise on Jewish law completed in the sixth century of the Common Era), law is a crucial tool in Judaism. Reflection on law leads to understanding; observance leads to virtue. But, above all, law can make a better world. Righting wrongs through law is an intrinsic part of the Jewish legacy to the West.

So is activism. Many Americans today seem to have an impatience for organized attempts to better the world. Maybe they are tired. Maybe they have been disappointed. They keep yelling, "Don't just do something. Sit there." Jewish tradition, on the contrary, is interventionist, from the grandmother who rushes over to check on the baby, to the thousands of schools and programs designed to create people who will make a difference. The tradition is not to just sit there. The Passover Haggadah, which tells the story of the Exodus out of Egypt, tells of four children who ask different questions. The fourth child, however, cannot even formulate a question. In that case, the Haggadah instructs, you begin the story for him. If something is that important, you do it. You don't wait for the question.

What is it that is important in the Jewish community? History. The story of past trials, past strengths, and how they speak to us today. In this sense affirmative action is morally right. It is an active effort to create a more just world through law by understanding history and its legacy. There are policy questions, and there is debate over the efficacy of various programs. Many, many observers have documented the need for affirmative action, especially the need to help women contribute as more equal members of this society. Other observers dispute the evidence. But who speaks to the American spirit, to our sense of passion and purpose?

Affirmative action is an important tool that can contribute toward and express our fundamental value of community. It is a way of fulfilling our social promises. As Americans, we added Constitutional amendments ensuring equality. But our Biblical ancestors understood that a promise is an important and fragile thing. The probability of fulfilling our promises is a function of the amount of time that elapses from the moment of the promise to its fulfillment. The longer we wait, the less likely the pledge will be fulfilled. Unless, of course, we make sure it is fulfilled. Deuteronomy says, "That which is gone out of thy lips thou shalt observe and do." Will we carry out our social promise, the promise of community?

You cannot reach community until you cross that river. Leave behind uncertainty. It is hard. Leave behind oppression. It is hard. The whole point is the struggle, and it is hard. God protected Joshua and his Hebrew armies when they crossed the Biblical Jordan, but there was a battle waiting for them on the other side. Americans have crossed their own Jordans but still found a battle on the other side. The African-Americans who went North left behind slavery and Jim Crow, but too often found the devastation of ghetto life, unemployment, and scorn. Yet they dared to dream and hope and succeed. And the European immigrants? The other great movement of people in the middle of our nation's history? They were poor. They were sick. The resurgence of tuberculosis in recent days is a grim reminder of earlier TB epidemics in crowded, dark tenements and the establishment of health codes early in the twentieth century.

At the same time, most of us know from personal family experiences that something worked. Ellis Island immigrants came in huge numbers, making America a virtual society of immigrants, each of whom had begun life anew, on equal footing. Maybe that was what gave America a renewed dedication to its old value, equality. The immigrants came with the fresh memory of old traditions, and an eagerness to explore new frontiers, a combination of strength and energy. If this century was going to prove a battle, they were prepared for it. And somehow the descendants of former slaves and the descendants of former peasants and ghetto-dwellers have given us a vigorous, energetic nation, strong and optimistic, graceful and daring. You have to admit, when community works, it is magnificent. The point is to have more of it, not less. If American music is unique now, with its rhythms and cadences of a hundred peoples, how much more spectacular is it when sung by so many different peoples? If American literature is compelling now, with its inner conflicts and outward cries, how much more compelling will it be when the stories multiply and the themes reverberate? When we cross that river to the future, it will be a pluralistic future. To remain isolated would not only be wrong; it would be boring.

THE RIO GRANDE

The American story has not ended; too many people act as if it has. All over America people are closing up shop, shutting down hopes, declaring the day finished and closing their hearts. They see shocking acts of terrorism and shutter the windows. They see financial woes and budget cuts and bar the gates. Too many Americans are blaming immigrants for their frustrations. Too many people have become suspicious of outsiders. Too many people accuse immigrants of draining our economy, filling our prisons, hurting our environment, destroying our schools. Hostility leads to violence and vicious assault.

We have forgotten that America is a country endlessly reinventing itself, working the alchemy that turns "them" into "us." Some fear that our newest immigrants, especially Asians and Latinos, cannot weave into the fabric of American culture. Too many people have come to see the world of the immigrant as dark and sinister—the ominous otherness, not "our" kind. This reaction is rooted in a fear of the unknown, the unfamiliar, fear of a new population challenging or eclipsing the present ethnic mix. But surrendering to the darkness of xenophobia is a mistake.

The immigrant holds an important place in our history and in our understanding of who we are. All of us. Franklin Delano Roosevelt once began an address to the Daughters of the American Revolution, "My fellow immigrants . . ." An immigrant is a seeker, a pilgrim. A sojourner. Abraham, instructed by God to leave his home and set off in the desert, was a traveler. Saul of Tarsus, on the road to Damascus, was a traveler. At one time or another we are all strangers, seeking something more in life. The problem is, we forget that feeling and settle into the world not as we find it, but as it finds us. We forget to make choices or even that there are choices. The question is not whether immigrants can be assimilated, but rather: Do they enrich or impoverish our nation? It is the immigrant who reminds us that we have choices. It is the immigrant who brings renewal and who reminds us to keep seeking.

Immigrants renew our population, adding young, strong workers to an aging country. Immigrants renew the economy of our cities, adding small businesses and revitalizing neighborhoods. What is more, immigrants renew our image of ourselves, helping us discover new aspects of America, both good and bad. A Jewish proverb says, "Who discovered the water? Certainly not the fish." The newcomer sees the world in a new way. Rather than presenting new problems, more often the newcomer can bring new solutions to old problems. One hundred years ago America's English speakers feared that immigrants would destroy the government, the landscape, and the language. Instead they and their grandchildren became avid Republicans and Democrats, both, impassioned environmentalists, and the most demanding of high school English teachers. But there is more.

Immigrants renew our values and remind us to rededicate ourselves to the ideals we hold. Their necessity for family help and cohesion reminds us that we, too, benefit from family support. Their determined efforts to study and succeed remind us that we, too, value learning and achievement. Their sacrifice and dogged determination to work remind us that we, too, can work hard and do well. Their mistakes make us laugh at our own. One self-taught immigrant, proud of his new language, addressed a large audience: "The other speakers have spoken to you only in vague generalities. But I'm going to speak to you at random!" And, you know, you have to nod with a smile at this unplanned truth. We do sometimes speak at random, don't we?

Of all the contributions immigrants make to our spiritual life, their greatest is simply being here. Their very lives attest to the human ability to start again, to seek, to hope, to face the future. While many older Americans fear for their children's future, many new Americans come specifically to give their children a future. They bring hope because they believe in hope. If they didn't, they wouldn't be here.

Renewal and community go together. The rhythm of life, with its seasons and births and deaths, is the natural province of religion. Some times are easy and joyful, and religion expresses that joy. Some times are difficult, and religion eases the pain. In our shared tradition the renewal of a new year or a new spring or a new life is cause for celebration. When a Jewish baby is named or an Episcopalian baby christened, the community begins again, enriched with a new member, just as the baby begins her own brand-new life.

The vigor and longevity of Catholic tradition has been closely tied to this idea of renewal. The Catholic Church in America has been a church of immigrants, from the large wave of Irish who came a hundred and fifty years ago after the Potato Famine to the Latinos who are arriving today. The Church worked on the newcomers' behalf to ensure that the new Americans had a chance. It was the strong-willed archbishop of New York, John Hughes, nicknamed "Dagger John," who insisted that a bank be founded to help the hundreds of thousands of victims of the Irish Potato Famine who poured into New York's slums. The Irish immigrants were cheap labor, easy prey for gougers and exploiters. The new Emigrant Industrial Savings Bank in Lower Manhattan opened on September 30, 1850, to provide a safe place for the newcomers to put their wages and a way to send money home. And just as the Church helped these newcomers start new lives, each group of immigrants gave new life to the Church. With traditional fervor they dedicated their sons to the priesthood. They made Catholicism part of the American landscape. The small Catholic churches founded by Polish immigrants to Pittsburgh do not resemble San Francisco's Mission Dolores, where Latinos pray. The worshippers do not eat the same food; they do not even celebrate all the same holidays. They do not speak the same language. What they share is the belief that they can start anew and that Catholicism can help them do that.

The most powerful Christian celebration of renewal is the celebration of Easter, the resurrection of Jesus Christ. Children may love Christmas, with its sense of excitement, surprise, and beginnings, but adults are often more moved by the drama of crucifixion and resurrection and by its promise of redemption. There was a Philippine immigrant to the United States, a devout and loving Catholic, whose family made a good beginning in this new country. One son became a manager for Pacific Bell Telephone. One daughter became a teacher. His wife had been a teacher until her retirement. Then the head of the family grew old and got cancer. His stomach swelled to four times its size, and his pain was so intense that he drifted in and out of consciousness. He lingered like this for months, approaching death. But he could not die, although everyone said their good-byes. Finally it was Good Friday, the day of Christ's crucifixion, and Good Friday allowed him to die. This man had believed that Jesus Christ was crucified so that He might live again in greater glory and so that humanity might find communion with God. So he hoped that his own life might have had some meaning, that he might live again in God. Because he was part of a community in God, the coming of Good Friday brought his release.

When Saint Thomas, Doubting Thomas, doubted the news of the Resurrection, he said, "I'll believe it when I see Jesus' hands and when I feel His side with my own hand." Think of the human hand. So serious. So industrious and concrete. Saint Thomas probably thought his very serious hand could tell him a very concrete truth. When the risen Christ appeared to him, though, and told Thomas to bring his hand over, that hand took on a different meaning. It was the hand offering God's love. Think of the human hand. So tender and expressive. Joining hands is an expression of community and of faith.

One of the most famous images of the human hand is in Michelangelo's depiction of the Creation on the ceiling of the Sistine Chapel in Rome, painted for Pope Julius II. God's hand reaches down toward Adam, whose hand in turn reaches up toward God's hand. The image of these reaching hands, so familiar in our visual vocabulary, expresses many things. It is Creation, new life. It is also re-creation or renewal, for while God is reaching down, Adam is also reaching up again and again, as often as we look, receiving again and again the spark that gave him life. And since humans were created in God's image, God's hand looks like a human hand. It is almost as if each time someone reaches out to another hand, he is reaching out to God.

Michelangelo knew the power of his painting and the power of all painting to express human feeling. Once a friend remarked on a certain artist's ability to render such a lifelike ox, and Michelangelo quipped, "Don't you know that all artists excel in self-portraits?" But on another occasion his friend, Vasari, asked the old Michelangelo, "Won't you miss painting? Won't you miss life when you die?" Michelangelo answered, "I have enjoyed life. And Death? Isn't that a work by the same Master?"

When a person dies, he dies alone. When he is a member of a community, although he dies his life is renewed. People remember him. Children follow him. Others follow his teachings or see his works. And if there were no one, no family, no memories, no teachings, a stranger could come upon his remains and imagine his life. That is what it means to be part of the human community. That is why we value community. We need a link to other human beings. We're not sure yet what that link is. But we know it's there.

Because we feel that link, we must do everything possible to open ourselves to other people. Open to others, we live as human beings. Closed and apart, we die as animals, alone, isolated. Those things that close the hearts of men and women, like racism and xenophobia, are wrong. And so in our shared tradition, we cry out for actions and behaviors that will keep our hearts open and expand our community. Out of a sense of history, justice, and a hope for renewal, we cry out for a more open American community. Affirmative action and broad immigration open our community to the talents and ideas of as many people as possible, large numbers and new talents.

We would like just laws, so that the powerless are not exploited and brown skin is not the sign of a second-class citizen.

We would like compassionate laws, so that people who have worked hard their whole lives can receive the benefits due them, whether or not they are voting citizens, because they are part of our American community, an open and caring community.

We don't say these things because they would make extraordinary laws; we support them because they are right. We are a community with a conscience, and we will defend the children of those who don't resemble us or think like us or speak like us.

Once, near another river, the Nile, a nation's immigrants faced threats. The Egyptian Pharoah ordered the killing of newborn Jewish males, thousands of years ago. He did it to prevent insurrection, to keep the peace, in other words, to keep Egypt for the Egyptians. Perhaps he distrusted their foreign language. Perhaps he thought too many had come into his country. Perhaps he wanted to discourage others from coming. Two brave midwives, Shifra and Puah, refused to kill the babies. They did not fear for the future; they wanted only to do what was right.

If the Delaware River showed us uncertainty and the Jordan showed us tyranny, what does the Rio Grande show us but fear of the future? If you look at that river with fear, you shrivel with hatred and isolation. If you look at it with hope, you see an America waiting to be made. Which will it be?

IV

Climbing Mountains

*There is fear where there
should be faith.*

Consider the tale of Saint Julian Hospitator whose hard-won faith moved him to share the suffering of an outcast.

Saint Julian Hospitator killed his parents. It was in that age of noblemen and hunting and great tapestries hung on massive stone walls, the fairy-tale time of dark forests and long-held secrets. So maybe it would be better to say that he broke his parents' hearts, since that is the way we say it today. His remorse knew no limits. He considered killing himself, but realized that such an act would be no more than a repetition of his horrible crime. So he abandoned his life of nobility and gave up his identity and disappeared into the forest.

Now, his life as young nobleman had been a life of conquest and carnage. He was a master of the hunt and laid whole forests bloody with the fruits of his slaughter. Then he rose to prominence as a soldier and laid armies waste. But in the forest, on the contrary, he did nothing but serve others as a ferryman. Despair taught him patience. Patience taught him mystery. Mystery taught him faith. He no longer thought he knew his future. He no longer thought his parents had known his future, or that their expectations for him were necessarily true. His crime was finished.

One day a leper whom Julian had ferried across the river demanded food, drink, and the warmth of Julian's body. Julian warmed the leper, who then changed appearance. His eyes shone like stars, his hair spread out like the rays of the sun. As he held tight to Julian, he grew and grew until the hut could no longer contain his radiance. The leper became the Lord Jesus Christ, who took Saint Julian Hospitator up toward the blue, to Heaven, and redemption.

And that is the legend of Saint Julian Hospitator, more or less as it is recounted in a tale told by Gustave Flaubert in a book of three tales.

❧

FAITH IS BELIEF IN THE REALM BEYOND WHAT CAN BE experienced. You cannot see it, hear it, taste it, smell it, or touch it. You have never seen it happen before; you have no reason to think it will happen now. Julian did not really know that caring for others would free him of his despair. He just believed it. His parents had never seen a child of theirs achieve either imperial might or sainthood. And they certainly never feared for themselves at the hands of their son. A parent has faith in a child, a believer has faith in God, a romantic has faith in love, the weak have faith in heroism, and the strong in compassion. It is such a rich world, this world of the invisible. When you think about it, we cannot see or hear or touch many of the most important things in our lives.

Of all the traditional values, Americans have taken faith as their own. The Pilgrims landed with nothing but a belief in Providence. Immigrants arrived with no more than a hope for the future. Statesmen designed a government they had never seen in practice. Experiment more often than experience has guided pioneers, industrialists, even presidents. When the Reverend Dr. Martin Luther King Jr. said that he had been to the mountaintop, when he described a world where black and white lived side by side in freedom, that was a supreme statement of faith. He himself had not seen that world in practice, nor had his listeners. It was his faith in that future world that gave him the strength to fight for justice. Faith has made Americans strong. And daring. Fred Astaire leaps from one step to another and for one brief second there is nothing holding him up but American optimism. Americans smile. We look for a smile in return. It is not arrogance; it is not foolishness. It is faith.

Americans still depend on large doses of faith. We believe

that some future technology will set us free, even though we have yet to meet the machine that can manufacture happiness. We believe the more leisure the better, even though we are always trying to determine what to do once we get that extra time. Americans invest and save, albeit less than the citizens of other nations. We vote, although there, too, the voter turnout here is not as great as in other countries.

The sociologist Daniel Bell was once asked to predict the American future, a request he did not relish since he distrusted "futurologists." He responded, "I predict that there will be a presidential election in 1980, another in 1984, another in '88, again in '92 and then a presidential election in 1996 and all the way up to the year 2000. A trivial observation? On the contrary. The fact that I can 'predict' that with certainty is one of the most fundamental facts about American democracy." At this fundamental level the country works, and Americans have faith in the system.

In recent days, and in many ways, however, faith has been replaced by fear. Who now has faith in American law enforcement or justice after being shocked by one trial after another? Thirty years ago the beloved Harlem congressman Adam Clayton Powell Jr. said, "Keep the faith, baby." Today many Americans live with fear daily. In some neighborhoods the fear of gunshots is a part of their daily life. In most neighborhoods people live with doubt. What will happen to them if they become sick? Will there be jobs for them next year? In five years? For their children?

Americans say, "Show me." We don't care very much for the invisible these days. "Show me the numbers. How do I know your projects will work? Exactly how many children benefited from Project Head Start, and on what days and with what reading scores?" People fear they are unable to make judgments. People fear contradictory answers. People fear being duped. Faith in all institutions—government, religion, schools, marriage, the press, the family, the workplace, the neighborhood, even friendship—has declined.

The long, slow decline of American faith was apparent in the Watergate scandal and the war in Vietnam. Not only did the government of Richard Nixon move away from the popular will and engage in covert action, provoking cynicism and alienation; the American people themselves became so sharply divided that neighbors eyed one another with distrust. Was Vietnam a generational war, in which eighteen-year-olds died while fifty-year-olds voted? Was it a race war, where black and Latino men fought while white men were "deferred"? Was it a political war, where followers said "enough," and leaders said "not on my watch"? The Establishment, the military-industrial complex, the bigness of it all, the impersonality—can you have faith in a nine-digit number?

Every so often observers have declared the end of Vietnam paralysis or Vietnam cynicism. Americans have since fought on other fronts, sent by leaders who wanted to prove themselves past Vietnam. No new sense of purpose has inspired us, however. On the contrary, recent developments have made Americans question all but their most immediate experiences. One of these is the growth of digital technology, rendering messages faster and higher quality, but not more truthful. One day it's morning in America and the next day you find out the rooster was reading from a teleprompter and had his comb done by Olaf of Hollywood. Onscreen people can now look perfect. But you know they're not. Or are they? Businesses can monitor world events more quickly than governments. Individual computer hackers can get to the battlefront faster than generals can.

The battlefront. It is a saddening, sobering fact that the widespread defeat of Communism has not resulted in universal peace, but in myriad ethnic conflicts and in particular the long, tragic, genocidal war in Bosnia. For years Americans believed and hoped for the defeat of Communism. Now it is defeated, or seems so, despite some Communist Party resurgence. What is our purpose? When Communism fell, tragedy followed. Was our faith misplaced? The Communist regime in Yugoslavia had at least forced peace on its populace. Someone once asked a rabbi, "Why is the Torah scroll always flanked by ferocious-looking lions? Whenever they build an ark to hold the Torah, they always seem to build on those vicious lions." The rabbi said, "Those are the lions of Judah. They remind us that were it not for the law, they would tear one another to pieces."

Is there a message here for America, too? If so, it is a frightening one, and we are afraid. What if, at some very deep and fundamental level, people feel such hatred for one another that an America is an impossibility? What if we are just too different to live together? The old American faith is gone; there is no comfort in conformity. We used to say, America alone together; we are the same in our difference from the rest of the world. Some people still say it. Today's religious right wing refuses to look outside the United States for lessons of hope. But the rest of us must look. Are there lessons we can learn from Bosnia? Can we learn from Burma? Is there a faith that unites us with other peoples?

Faith need not be single, uniform, and conformist. Conformity is not comfortable, after all. Faith is diffuse, multiple, even contradictory. Just as Saint Julian Hospitator's father dreamed of war and his mother dreamed of peace, we have different faiths, different systems that keep us grounded. Anyone can have faith. Saint Julian Hospitator found it when he needed it. Faith is confidence in life. It comes first and last, at times ordinary and extreme, in settings public and private.

FIRST AND LAST

> *You shall love the Lord your God with all your mind, with all your strength, with all your being. Set these words, which I command you this day, upon your heart. Teach them faithfully to your children; speak of them in your home and on your way, when you lie down and when you rise up. Bind them as a sign upon your hand; let them be a symbol before your eyes; inscribe them on the doorposts of your house, and on your gates.*

Sometimes faith comes first. Sometimes the faith has to be there before you can even begin. We teach faith to children to give them this start. Claude G. Montefiore said, "I do not pretend to understand how the divine Creator influences the human child . . . [T]he influences of spirit make their way in different degrees, or not at all, to different souls." But we teach faith because sometimes it is faith that pushes us into action.

The Jesuit thinker and scientist Pierre Teilhard de Chardin, believed that it is a person's duty to throw himself into the world, to turn faith into action. In the early and middle years of this century he researched as a paleontologist, struggled as a philosopher, and debated as a supporter of faith against existential despair. He never argued faith against science, though. For him faith preceded science. Armed with faith one examines the wonders of the universe. (First.) Faith also followed science. (And last.) Armed with the lessons of science, the scientist sees the world as increasingly wonderful.

Albert Einstein, master physicist of our century, expressed the scientist's faith in order and beauty: he believed that God would not play dice with the universe. Einstein also expressed his faith in faith over observation: Once, crossing the Princeton campus, he ran into a colleague and lost himself in a few minutes of conversation. As the conversation ended he looked bewildered. "Which way was I going?" he asked his friend. The colleague smiled and pointed. "That way; you were going in that direction when we ran into one another." "Ah, good," Einstein is said to have said. "Then I've already eaten lunch." Full stomach? Empty stomach? Mere empiricism. Follow the path and find the meaning.

Theoretical scientists like Teilhard de Chardin or Einstein often see wonder and meaning at the end of the scientific path. Even those who do not, however, have faith in faith. Faith is like a hypothesis, a guess about the world, and scientists work in hypotheses, even if these hypotheses are at times competing or contradictory. One visitor to Niels Bohr's lab was shocked to see a horseshoe hanging on the physicist's wall. "You? Superstitious?" the visitor cried. "Oh, no," Bohr responded lightly. "I hear it works even if you don't believe in it."

First and last, beginning and end, alpha and omega. Sometimes the scientist's original wonder reappears at research's end. Sometimes the rote faith of childhood takes on meaning and reappears only after adult experience. Sometimes when you lie down at the end of the day, grateful for a good day passed, you remember your anxiety when you rose in the morning and the strength that allowed you to begin. Sometimes you leave your doorposts and your gates with nothing but high hopes, and you return to those gates and doorposts and understand how hope got you through your errand.

But sometimes faith comes last. You did your errand. You did one thousand errands. Each of those individual errands was right or good or important to you. You visited a sick friend. You gave some money to charity. You just did what you thought made sense. Faith? Maybe you never thought about it. Maybe it sounded silly or mystical. You just lived what looked like a decent life, trying to make the world a better place. Then on the thousand and first errand you said, "Aaaaah."

According to the writer Arthur Koestler, there are three types of insights. They can come from hearing stories, but they also come from living experiences. A simple "Ha, ha," means you get the joke. An "Ah, ha," means you've drawn the conclusion. But when you say "Aaaaaah," you have made a bigger connection. You have drawn a lesson about life. On the thousand and first errand you say, "Aaaaah." *This* is the meaning. I have been following some purpose. I see the pattern. Like the character in Moliere's play who is thrilled to discover he has been speaking prose his entire life, a person finds pattern and meaning at last. Then faith follows understanding.

So is faith based on wonder or understanding? Is it mystery or science? Is it the gift of a child or the reward of an aged soul? Does one love life at its beginning, when all is new, or at its end, when all is precious? All of these. Faith is the freedom to stop asking impossible questions and to focus on the possible. Faith frees you to enjoy life. Faith frees you to fight for what is right. Faith frees you to explore.

But the shape of that faith, the style, the timing, the content? It is diverse, multiple, personal, cultural. You choose. We will be honest. Faith is a difficult subject because faith takes many forms, and we have different faiths. Faith is tested. The book of Proverbs says that an exemplary person "laughs at the time to come." That is one kind of faith—an utter confidence that finds the world undaunting. Our shared tradition values confidence. In Yiddish its extreme is called *chutzpah*. The trial lawyer and author Alan Dershowitz, a master of *chutzpah*, gives this definition: it is when a man charged with the murder of both his parents throws himself at the court's mercy as an orphan. This is the same confidence that laughs at death; it is the unswerving belief that the outcome will be good, that there will be rewards to come.

In Episcopalian life independent action and a willingness to take risks require confidence and a belief in a good outcome. The message of the sure hope of glory inspires change and action. The qualities that accompany confidence, such as poise and grace, also go along with faith. The Anglican gentleman's stiff upper lip is an expression of faith in a just world and a good outcome, rewards for the just and decent.

Grace and beauty go along with the lilies of the field, who "toil not, nor do they spin," confident that God will care for them. In their faith is their beauty. Jesus said,

> Behold the fowls of the air: for they sow not, neither do they reap, nor gather into barns; yet your heavenly Father feedeth them. Are ye not much better than they? . . . Consider the lilies of the field, how they grow; they toil not, neither do they spin. . . .
>
> Wherefore, if God so clothe the grass of the field, which to day is, and to morrow is cast into the oven, *shall he* not much more clothe you, O ye of little faith?

But very few of us really laugh at the time to come or disregard tomorrow. The world is so full of tests of faith. For the Catholic, the essence of faith is belief in the primary importance of the life of the spirit. The material world, though, distracts and disturbs. All of us, living in community, find life with others a trial. We hurt when our children are chosen last for a team, when they don't get a part in a play, when they are rarely invited to parties or are rejected by their peers. We don't necessarily trust in good outcomes, but we want to protect our children from life's harsher side. Like Laban.

Laban had two daughters, Rachel, who was beautiful, and Leah, who was older and not very beautiful. Jacob wanted to marry the beautiful Rachel and struck a deal with her father. Jacob was to work for seven years to earn the right to marry her. When the seven years passed, Laban appeared to be living up to his bargain. Yet when Jacob awoke the morning after the wedding, he found that his veiled bride was Leah, not Rachel.

Although Laban rationalized his deceit by saying, "It is not the practice in our place to marry off the younger before the older," his words reflect much more than social convention. He took to heart the plight of his unattractive, awkward daughter. Any parent who has hoped to see his or her child find a mate or success in life can relate to Laban's concern for his daughter.

Still Laban couldn't give Leah a happy life. Her husband didn't love her and never loved her, even after she had given birth to six children. Imagine her parents looking on and experiencing her heartache. In spite of all her unhappiness, Leah was still able to shoulder her burdens, find the good in her life, and discover rewards for her endurance and faith. Although hers is a sad tale, a story of deceit, manipulation, and disappointment, it is also a story about a test of faith when children disappoint us, parents disappoint us, or the world itself seems out of kilter.

ORDINARY AND EXTREME

Our Father who art in heaven
Hallowed be thy name.
Thy Kingdom come. Thy will be done
On Earth as it is in heaven.
Give us this day our daily bread
And forgive us our trespasses
as we forgive those who trespass against us.
And lead us not into temptation,
but deliver us from evil:
For thine is the kingdom, and the power, and the glory,
for ever and ever. Amen.

Give us this day our daily bread. Most of us would love a lightning bolt or two. A sign, but a really big sign. If not Saint Paul's conversion on the road to Damascus, then at least a really good, modern, existential abyss and the ability to make one magnificent leap. If faith is a gift, we want it all at once, all wrapped up, presented with a drumroll. A bona fide miracle. But such a spectacle is very rare. For most of us faith is a lifelong passage from one ordinary day to the next, each day a very tiny ordinary miracle of daily bread, a little belief at a time. Some miracles are too small to see; some miracles are too big to see; some don't look like miracles. Moses took his people out of Egypt amid the most amazing wonders and signs, including the parting of the Red Sea. The people were saved. And then, in the desert, when life was hard and food scarce, the people turned to idols and false gods and away from the God of Moses. "How could they?" Moses said in his anguish. "Did they forget? Did they never believe? Did they not believe their own history?" For most of us, the Red Sea does not part every day, and the faith of ordinary life is small and quiet.

At the same time, ordinary life can be an extraordinary source of faith. The nineteenth-century Oxford poet and Jesuit Gerard Manley Hopkins wrote, "The world is charged with the grandeur of God," and he described nightfall, the stormy sea, the mossy bank, the unfolding rose, all details of Nature infused with purpose and beauty, or Grace. What could be more ordinary than the simple biological fact of the birth of a baby? Millions of babies are born every day. Yet for the parents that simple bit of nature seems extraordinarily beautiful and purposeful. Child development, too, follows a natural path—movement, speech, thought. Yet why should that path lead to moral reasoning, or idealism in an eighteen-year-old? The process of growing and developing is all very ordinary, yet it is a source of faith.

On the other hand, ordinary life is, well, ordinary. Saturday there is the soccer game and then dinner with the Smiths. No miracles lately. What do you do when having fun isn't fun anymore? Often it is the ordinariness of life that prompts people to look for meaning, to seek out some faith. Faith is that feeling of purpose and connectedness that gives ordinary life meaning. It is a last resort in a tired world of petty disappointments and empty promises.

Some disappointments, some sorrows and griefs and partings, are not small at all. In extreme circumstances, in extremis, faith grows strong. When the economy falters, more people attend religious services. Under hardship and persecution, faith may be the only freedom left to express. Faith is a kind of freedom. Belief in meaning and purpose sets people free to act and to work hard to survive. Faith and freedom, though, have an uneasy relationship. Once there is freedom to think, to write, to speak, to buy, to sell, to gather, churches and synagogues seem less important. Polish Catholicism flourished and strengthened under the Communist regime, which forbade religious worship. Polish Catholics' increased feeling of purpose and destiny allowed them to build a strong union movement, Solidarity, which eventually toppled the regime. With the end of Communism there is a freer Poland. And now the churches are no longer as central to people's lives.

The same movement away from faith takes place in the United States. Immigrants arrive ardent with devotion. After one or two generations they see that devotion is not crucial to survival in a country that is open and free. Not only that, the United States exports its brand of freedom. Thousands of the faithful flock to religious meetings in repressive China. But many people believe that even economic freedom, even a bottle of Coke, makes possible a freer and less religious life.

Is this an argument against faith and for freedom? Yes— against faith as a form of government. When it comes to earthly

power, the skepticism, doubt, and questioning associated with freedom are the best checks and balances. A country with an official,
institutionalized religious faith risks losing its faith or its freedom or
both. In Israel today Orthodox Judaism's official status has forced
many Jewish Israelis to choose between faith and freedom. It is a
rare balancing act, a unique achievement of the United States, that
there is separation of Church and State, there is no official religion
here, and that this country is both free and faithful. How do we do
that? Not by luck, not by coincidence, but by giving individuals the
freedom to choose their faith.

In grief and suffering we look for some help and guidance,
and the freedom to seek such support is a fundamental human necessity.

> *My delight is in the Lord*
> *   because he hath heard the voice of my prayer;*
> *Because he hath inclined his ear unto me,*
> *   therefore will I call upon him as long as I live.*
> *The snares of death compassed me round about,*
> *   and the pains of hell got hold upon me.*
> *I found trouble and heaviness;*
> *   then called I upon the Name of the Lord;*
> *   O Lord, I beseech thee, deliver my soul.*
> *Gracious is the Lord, and righteous;*
> *   yea, our God is merciful*
> *The Lord preserveth the simple;*
> *   I was in misery and he helped me.*

Death, the most extreme of all circumstances, is frightening. It is
true that much of life is hard, but so much of life is so beautiful, so
filled with grandeur, so amazing. The thought that it will all disappear is painful. The thought that nothing endures is painful.

The Lord is my shepherd,
    I shall not want.
He makes me lie down in green pasture,
    He leads me beside still waters.
He restores my soul. He leads me in the right paths for
        the sake of His name. Even when I walk in the valley
        of the shadow of death, I shall fear no evil, for You
        are with me; with rod and staff You comfort me. You
        have set a table before me in the presence of my enemies;
        You have anointed my head with oil, my cup overflows.
Surely goodness and mercy shall follow me all the days of my
        life and I shall dwell in the house of the Lord for ever.

Grief is a teacher. It teaches us to comfort others. It teaches us silence and humility in the face of others' sorrow. Saint Julian Hospitator's grief taught him to serve and care for others. He didn't really know why he hurt his parents. It was part accident, part prophecy, partly the natural outcome of his early life. He had no release from his grief until he let it teach him to trust the future.

The gay community has been confronted by the most extreme circumstances in the form of the AIDS epidemic, and as a result that community has become galvanized politically, culturally, and religiously. Most of us know in general the broad swath of death the human immunodeficiency virus cut through American life. A generation of dancers, choreographers, writers, set designers, fashion designers, and actors have been stolen from the American arts. Historians, community activists, journalists, and civil servants will no longer be lending their voices to our civic discourse. This is all in the newspapers. The obituaries of some of America's best and brightest have replaced announcements of awards for achievements. We know the effect this plague has had on America. The effect on individuals has been even more staggering. One gay man said that he personally watched forty people die. In this context loved ones think about memory, grief, and what it means to endure.

Gays have found faith in the truth that memory survives. The NAMES Project or the AIDS Memorial Quilt, records the names and lives of the dead to show that they will not be forgotten. In our shared religious tradition, each individual human being is of worth and significance; no one is lost and everyone matters. We draw comfort and strength from the belief that everyone matters.

Gays have found faith in community. Friends and acquaintances who survive not only ease the sharpest grief, but promise that someone will be there to remember the dead. An outpouring of literary and artistic works on the subject of AIDS not only explores the subject but expresses the community. Gay men and lesbians can now feel connected to a literature and worldview softened by sympathy and grief and strengthened by shared experience.

Gays have found faith in political action. They now live with hope that the future will bring civic equality. They long for the freedom to live as all free Americans live, and like all Americans they are partners in the same great paradox of freedom and faith. They long to be free to believe and also to share that precious democratic gift of skepticism. They have faith in civic recognition.

Gays have faith that a cure for AIDS will be found in the future. No one has seen the cure so far. In fact, experience has shown only some advances. The belief in the human ability to completely solve scientific problems, however, is a powerful one. So is the scientific belief in order, the belief in a just and loving God, and the belief in Nature and Grace. All of these ideas point to a cure for this disease. The faith on this issue is a strong and powerful faith and a life-affirming one. Signs declare, BE HERE FOR THE CURE.

Yet for gays and lesbians in America there is still a lot to fear. Whereas heterosexuals experience the glow of their parents' faith in them, many homosexuals do not. They wonder, How will my parents respond to me? Will they accept me as a human being, as one of God's creations? Or will they turn away as if from an ugly, unwanted thing? If they do accept me, will they dream for me the same dreams they would dream for any child, dreams of love and affection? Or will they shut down their dreams and see only a shadow child whose inner life means nothing to them?

Faith does not come easily to these gays and lesbians. Whether or not they believe in God or believe that God cares for them, many of them face religious traditions that do not welcome them as worshippers. For them, then, faith is an uphill climb in the best of circumstances. There are gay religious groups, but for the most part religious ritual is closed to most gays. The custodians of the realm of the ultimate have not bid them enter.

America's religious institutions have responded nobly and wholeheartedly to the AIDS crisis with meals, hospice care, and healing services. At the same time, there is still reason for gays to fear, asking themselves, "Am I worth more dead than alive? Why may I enter a holy place as a dying soul, yet I am told that I defile it as a living soul? Who am I, then, if I stand for death?"

In all of these ways, in all of these fears, AIDS has presented us with a crisis of the American spirit. The homosexual community has had to continually confront its fears and confirm its faith in the future. The heterosexual community needs to examine its own compassion and caring and clarify its expectations. One cannot enter a room if the door is locked. Do we want gays and lesbians in the room? If we do not, we cannot demand their presence. If we do, we must open the door. The room is faith. It is in a house with many mansions.

All three of our faiths have a strong element of sense and

sensuality. The Catholic and Anglican churches both believe in a Christ who walked on earth in blood and body, a God incarnate, who lived and died and suffered. The human form is essential to this understanding, and sexuality is part of the human form. In the English literary canon we meet Shakespeare's Hamlet who sums up the glory of the human form thus:

> What [a] piece of work is a man, how noble in reason, how infinite in faculties, in form and moving, how express and admirable in action, how like an angel in apprehension, how like a god! the beauty of the world; the paragon of animals.

The prince's melancholy prevents him from appreciating all this beauty, he admits, including the sex. "Man delights not me—nor women neither, though by your smiling you seem to say so," he chides his companion Rosencrantz. In centuries of painting and literature Western figures, including Biblical figures, appear as male and female. Even the births of Jesus and of his mother Mary, both conceived without human intercourse, according to Christian tradition, take place in the context of human sexuality: God implants them in the wombs of women, and they are born in the same way that all humans are born.

The Jewish tradition, if anything, is even more naturalistic in its sensuality. The Bible's Song of Songs, also called the Song of Solomon, is a poem of passion, desire, and physical possession, a poem prominent in Jewish tradition. King Solomon's beautiful bride, the Shulamite, avows, "I am my beloved's and my beloved is mine," for she is overcome, sick with love. But Solomon, too, a mighty king, is subject to the power of physical love.

> *Thou art beautiful, O my love, as Tirzah,*
> *Comely as Jerusalem,*

Terrible as an army with banners.
Turn away thine eyes from me,
For they have overcome me.

These images are living images; we live with them every day. It's the rare Jewish wedding that doesn't have at least one or two gifts inscribed, "I am my beloved's and my beloved is mine." It's the rare Episcopal gathering that doesn't boast a "handsome man of the room," a man noticed for his form and grace and presence. And according to the Catholic priest and sociologist Andrew Greeley, Catholics responding to confidential surveys are more likely than not to describe their sexual lives as fulfilling and exciting. Loving, sensual sex is a gift from God and an expression of God's love through His creations.

Beyond that our traditions part ways, and we speak not of souls, but of social actors. All human beings deserve respect, the right not to be ridiculed as well as the right to be ridiculous. The right to social justice: jobs, housing, health care. We know as well as anyone that people differ in their moral stance toward homosexuality. Within our own churches and synagogues there are moral and theological debates. Too often, though, the voice of the fundamentalist Right sounds a tone of ridicule or scorn. We cannot afford to scorn anyone. We have not a single human being to spare. Today AIDS is among the spiritual crises, and the fight for social justice falls to gays and lesbians. But tomorrow there will be more crises, and someone else will be moved to act. Is there anything we can learn to prepare us for the next fight?

Discoveries in biology and genetics are coming thick and fast. The Human Genome Project has mapped much of the human blueprint, describing the chromosomes responsible for congenital defects and fatal diseases. This is a good time to remember that we no more choose our bodies than we choose our parents. When faith is tested with the question, "Why me?" it is good to remember that in each of us there is a part that we cannot see. There is a part that cannot be mapped. In that part, we are all equals. Men must fight for women and women for men; homosexuals must help heterosexuals, and heterosexuals help homosexuals. For not one of us chooses the day and hour of our death. We are all equals there.

The fight against breast cancer and the urgency to find a cure is everyone's fight. Women in particular are moved to action because so many women are killed each year by this terrible disease. The fight, though, is society's fight. The individual suffers, the individual dies, but the fight is everyone's. Americans tend to blame each man or woman for his or her own death. We see the quaint image of someone with a knapsack chock full of the details of his days. He unpacks them: his habits, his diseases, his mistakes, his likes and dislikes. Then he packs them up and he is gone. "Poor old Fred," we say, "he packed up too soon," or "he packed too light," or "he packed too sloppy." That's where the image is wrong. Each of us may be given packs, but none of us knows what's in them. If we do, we don't know what it means. There is a mystery there we have yet to unravel.

One doctor commented, "Right now we don't consider it a medical problem if someone doesn't run fast. We know some of the chemical and structural elements that contribute to running fast. We don't know how to control them, though, and we just call it chance or luck. Someday we may know so much that slow running will be a treatable disease. And then what will we say about the time when it wasn't treated? Or, even more difficult, will we choose to treat it?"

There is so much we don't know about medicine, about the human body, about human sexuality. If we must err, let us err on the side of equality. If we must err, let us err on the side of kindness. If we must err, let us err on the side of the soul and the spirit and our best hopes. Then the beauty of form will delight us rather than control us, and the life of physical passion will be a joy to share, rather than a source of shame and degradation.

PUBLIC AND PRIVATE

> *We come ever closer together by our intimate talks.*
> *You tell Me your fears, worries, heartaches,*
>   *your joys, hopes, plans for the future.*
> *I listen to every word,*
>   *for whatever happens to you*
>   *happens to Me,*
> *and whatever anyone does to you in the least way*
>   *he does to Me.*
> *This is how close we are,*
> *You confide in Me and I confide in you.*
> *This is prayer.*

Just as there are many faiths and many forms of faith, there are many different expressions of faith. One expression of faith is action, or works, or deeds. Within the Catholic tradition, Jesuits are "contemplative in action": they express their beliefs in their deeds, which are rooted in prayer. Historically, they have founded schools or missions to express their faith.

In Jewish life prayer claims a place only alongside study and acts of loving kindness or charity. Conceptions of God and the requirements for serving God have been fluid and have evolved over the past five thousand years. Human sacrifice gave way to animal sacrifice; animal sacrifice gave way to symbolic sacrifice. Likewise the God who hears Jewish prayers has changed aspect as Jews have struggled to make sense of their history. Was the God who parted the Red Sea the same God whose creatures built Auschwitz? So many Jewish families were touched by the Holocaust that the particular struggle of faith it brought about is intensely personal.

Faith can be intensely personal. Individual Christians may feel close to God the Father, or close to the person of Jesus as a personal savior, one who speaks from the heart of God. A person may be moved by a sense of a more general goodness and spirituality in the world. This personal faith may be sung, shouted, danced, marched, hummed, meditated, or may simply radiate out from the person as confidence, happiness, or kindness. But of all the expressions of faith in the goodness of the world, perhaps the most common is prayer.

Prayer, the desire to speak to something beyond ourselves, seems to be universal among humans. Children play; souls pray. Souls pray to give thanks, to ask forgiveness, to express wonder, to strengthen their resolve, and to seek comfort in a bewildering world. The power of these feelings is so strong that rituals and holidays have been built to give voice to them. The Jewish holiday of Yom Kippur, the most important religious day of the year for most Jews, is devoted to saying, "I'm sorry"—an entire holiday to express and transcend regret. On that day repentance should be so sincere and so strong that individuals show physical change to show their new resolve, so interpretation says. Someone might stand straighter or smile or walk with confidence. Prayer can even be an avenue for change. On Ash Wednesday Catholics and Episcopalians take on a physical change, ash on their foreheads, to show the power of their repentance. During Lent, the period preceding Easter, Catholics and Protestants change their habits and their lives in order to strengthen their resolve, undertaking special study and assuming spiritual tasks.

There is something beyond personal faith and personal prayer. Yes, we pray to change. We pray for those we love. We pray that love will be stronger than death and that we will be remembered or that those we love will be remembered. But is there a way to get beyond prayer as a private possession? Can we get beyond prayer merely for ourselves or our group or our mission or our destiny or for those who seem to share our beliefs? A father complained to a rabbi that his son had forsaken God. "Rabbi, what shall I do?" The rabbi responded, "Love him more than ever." Prayer can be open and inclusive.

Prayer can be public. For centuries Catholics have gathered in public prayer to express togetherness, community, and equality in God's eyes. Public worship allows the individual to claim his or her place as a spiritual equal in society. A Polish Catholic in Brooklyn explained why he attends mass: "I am just a handyman. People criticize me, humiliate me. When I go to mass I reclaim my humanity. I am a human being again."

So if prayer is so remarkable and such a powerful and common expression of faith, should America require that its schoolchildren pray? In the past there was prayer in school. Worship in public schools was long the norm. Until 1963 the majority of American public school children were frequent participants in Bible readings and prayer recitations from Christian scripture, including the Lord's Prayer. In June of 1963 the U.S. Supreme Court ruled 8 to 1 that both practices are unconstitutional, arguing that the state should not compose or sponsor children's prayers.

Members of minority religions always found the prayers objectionable and unsettling. Even members of majority religions found that school prayer was a pale shadow of the real prayer, at church, where the words had meaning and not just cadence. It is not worth the bitter and hostile fight it would take to bring back school prayer as long as there is prayer in church. Prayer in public school simply is not necessary to a free and faithful America.

What about those who believe that deeds more truly express faith than prayer does? For them school prayer is not the antidote to society's collapse. In their view, educators should teach the universally shared values of honesty, decency, charity, appreciation of free speech and press, concern for the rights and freedoms of others, and respect for individuals from other ethnic and cultural backgrounds. And they should teach students how to apply these principles in their lives.

Even for those who believe in the strength of prayer, though, the American separation of church and state is too important to justify the intrusion of the government into the private world of faith. The framers of our Constitution had observed the cruelty of European nations toward minorities and dissenters. But they had also witnessed the behavior of some refugees from religious intolerance once they became powerful. For example, the Puritans—driven from England by the Anglicans—ruthlessly forced Baptists and Catholics, among others, out of colonial Massachusetts. They denied to others the freedom of worship for which they had zealously fought. Nonetheless this country's founders believed that an individual's right to religious liberty outweighed the will of the majority in religious matters. Governmental concessions to military chaplaincies, tax exemptions, postal privileges, and the deductibility of contributions to religious institutions are only signs of an uneasy alliance, never a collusion, between church and state.

Did we say that the world of faith is private? After arguing the importance of faith in American life, after claiming that fear has made us question our national mission and our relationships to one another, why would we insist that faith be private? Isn't faith a public good? Shouldn't it be shared?

Imagine a streetlight. It is a public good. Everyone benefits when the light is lit. There are fewer car accidents. People feel safe while strolling in the evenings. In the building on the corner, though, one man draws his shades. He has had a long and difficult day, and he would like to sleep. Certainly he is welcome to draw his shades. The light is there for him to enjoy, but he is not forced to enjoy it. Faith is like that light. Many can benefit from faith. A confidant and happy America would be more tolerant, open, and trusting. It would be cruel and absurd, though, to force anyone to feel faith. In the United States faith is both public and private. It is diverse, multiple, open to anyone—and forced on no one.

In what do Americans have faith? In a patriarch, in a matriarch, in a Great Spirit, in Order, Beauty, in Nature, in History, in a Supreme Being, a Holy Trinity. Faith itself has been removed from the monopoly of institutions and democratized, spread among the people freely, and they are free to enjoy it. We all share equally the freedom to believe, the freedom to express faith, and the freedom to trust. *"I will lift up mine eyes unto the hills, / from whence cometh my help."* Up, beyond ourselves. Up Saint Julian Hospitator rose toward the blue. Up toward the hills and mountains and away from this flat place.

TWO LAWYERS FIERCELY ARGUED THEIR CASE BEFORE a judge. The first was concise, sharp, and very convincing. The judge said, "You're right." The second lawyer rose to object. Her logic was subtle, refined, and indisputable. The judge said, "Hmm. Yes, you're right." This prompted an onlooker in the courtroom to shout in frustration, "But, your Honor, how could they both be right?" The judge thought for a moment. "Good point. You're right, too."

You might have noticed that so far everyone in this book is

"right." All ideas are good ideas, all traditions are "our shared" traditions, all values are good values. The common ground is the foreground, and the hazy no-man's-lands and disputed territories fall deep in the shadows. Any reader with a sharp eye and a cynical edge will grow restless. "What about . . . didn't they . . . I thought those people. . . . Aren't they the ones who . . ." As for such a cynic, he is right, too. Episcopalians, Jews, and Catholics have not always been in agreement. At times in history these groups have been at odds. Even now, when American life, liberty, and the pursuit of happiness bring members of these groups into more frequent contact, there are frictions and misunderstandings. We'd rather recap some important themes than explore the seamy underside. We do not claim that the three traditions are in perfect agreement, just that there is agreement enough.

First, the project of the American future is paramount in our thoughts. Our histories are very long, and our stories expand far beyond this continent. While those histories are important to us, our concern here is not the past, but the future, and not the whole world, but the United States. We speak as Americans to a nation of Americans. We speak of American values. Our search for agreement is not empty civility, but an act of desperate importance as we fight for what the economist John Kenneth Galbraith calls a more "humane agenda." We can't agree on everything, but we agree where it counts, on our goals for American society: a more compassionate, egalitarian, inclusive, peaceful, better-educated society.

We also share some basic religious beliefs. All three religions believe in an all-powerful deity. We share a belief in the goodness of life, the belief that life is valuable and should be cherished and preserved. We share the belief that human history will lead to perfection, that a better time will come. We work toward that time because we were given stewardship of the earth. We feel responsible.

We were entrusted with the resources, the ideas, the stuff of the earth. In addition to these very basic common beliefs, we share some other traits. We are three religious minorities within this country; granted, of different sizes, but minorities with distinctive histories.

The basic religious differences between us can be similarly summed up in simple phrases. Jews do not believe that Jesus Christ was the Messiah or God's messenger sent to redeem humankind. Catholics and Episcopalians do not believe that human beings are born blameless, but rather that they are cleansed through baptism. Our texts are different. Our customs are different. Our holidays are different.

So let's return to our two lawyers. How do you make a case in a courtroom where everyone's right? Or, to put it another way, How can you incorporate all peoples, allow for differences, recognize disagreements, avoid old wounds and also face the future, forge alliances, set goals, and make choices?

A very American question that.

Maybe the courtroom image isn't apt. It might call for a different, less shrill style of advocacy.

V

Through Forests

*There is exploitation where
there should be awe.*

Here the earth begins for us.

ROOTS

In the beginning, before there were people, there was the Earth. There was land before there were people; there was day and night, light and dark, trees and flowers, beasts and birds. All of these things came first. And because they came first, their origin is a source of wonder to us. Human beings have spent all of their thousands of years of existence puzzling over what we call the natural world. Because we just weren't here first.

So in this chapter we may very well meet some interesting individuals. We may hear their stories or recount their anecdotes or struggle over their dilemmas. But no individual human struggle begins this chapter, because that was not how it began. The Earth was here first.

Like an older brother or sister, the Earth asserts its primacy. Every so often it reminds us of our puny stature with an earthquake or a flood. But for the most part we younger siblings lord it over nature with bravado, and often the plants and animals and the Earth let us. We are the brash latecomers, full of ideas, full of energy, full of fight. We cut down forests and muddy rivers and blacken winds. Like a patient older sibling, the Earth has let us expend our energy. Now the time has come due to defer. It is time to see the Earth not as an older brother there to take the punches, but as an older brother there to be cherished, honored, and loved. It is time to express our wonder, declare our admiration, admit our smallness and honestly agree—we just weren't here first. This wonder and amazement and admiration we'll call awe.

Our spiritual life is linked to our experience of the natural world. It's more than in the words we use to describe our physical surroundings, although the only words we know are *universe* and *heavens, mountains* and *rivers*. We describe revelation as a burning bush. And the only way we know to describe that inner place where you face yourself all alone, where, as when you are fighting addiction, you face a challenge to your very core, the only way we know to express that is the idea of wilderness. "Consider the lilies of the field." "I am my beloved's . . . his eyes are like doves." "The kingdom of heaven is like a grain of mustard seed." "The wolf shall dwell with the lamb." "And all shall sit under his fig tree." The Bible uses the images and metaphors of plants and animals of the natural world to give voice to our deepest feelings, to express our needs, and to explain our human experience. These are our words. Were we to lose the reality, our words would sound empty. If no wolf walked the earth, would we really understand Isaiah's vision of peace, as the wolf and lamb dwelling together? If no mustard plants grew, would we lose Jesus' meaning of magnitude and glory? It's hard to say. Words, like species, can become extinct. But it's not just the words that are important.

Some of our deepest spiritual experiences are experiences of the natural world. Nature fills us with awe, first because it shows us longevity and reminds us of our own brief time here. In China there is a mission hundreds of years old. It attests to hundreds of years of history. Next to it is a gingko tree much older by far. The mission is impressive, but the tree is awe inspiring. How many generations has it watched come and go? How many lovers marveled that their love would look at the same tree and whispered to the tree, "Remember"? And now we look at the tree and recall all the lovers, all the history, so long ago. We realize, sadly, that we will not be here long, and we are tempted to tell the tree—or the stone—"Remember." It is a Jewish tradition to place stones or pebbles on a gravestone to mark a visit. When we are gone, the stones of this place will remember. And if there were no more stones? If there were only man-made houses and man-made vehicles and a man-made life? Then who or what would remember for us? Our understanding of longevity would be lost and our spirit crushed. And we ourselves would lose our ability to remember, with no place to help us whisper.

Nature fills us with awe because it shows us magnitude and reminds us of our smaller place in the Creation. With the help of computers human beings can count grains of sand, number the stars, and calculate beyond our own abilities. But for most of us, every day, the grains of sand go uncounted and the stars are too many to number. It shocks us to hear that there are thousands of kinds of beetles. It is impossible to hold all of nature in mind at once. It is so vast. Even imagining the Alaskan wilderness is a difficult stretch for most of us, for whom the largest forests they have seen are in national parks, and even those they saw only a part of. Close your eyes and imagine one hundred trees. Now two hundred trees. One thousand. At what point does the number of trees become blurry and indistinct? You have stopped counting. If you are tired, you'll fall asleep. If alert, you'll feel anxious. Most of us find nature too big to master. When we stop counting and admit our insignificance, we learn a spiritual lesson. And if the magnitude were diminished? What if only two beetles had to stand in for the thousands, and one potted geranium represented spring? Our understanding of magnitude would be lost and our spirit crushed.

Nature fills us with awe because it shows us quiet and reminds us of our piercing cacophony. The human voice is magnificent. It is grand, tender, moving, melodic, efficient, and exact all at once. Our days are filled with human voices and with the voices of our machines. It can become too much. We are so moved by our own voices that they echo in our brains. There are so many voices reverberating there that we sometimes barely hear or listen to anything else. Your own voice narrates your feelings and desires and ideas. The voice of authority tells you what to do. The voices of your family and friends impress their opinions on you. By the time you face the world outside you, you are not listening, for the noise of your life. In nature your voice is hushed. Sometimes there are no human voices at all. The quiet reminds you to listen. Sitting quietly is not only a way to renew your own spirit; it is a way to awaken to the spirits of others. The screech owl of the forest demands attention, and the cricket yells, "Listen here. Listen here." After a time when you meet another human voice, your ears are keened and your mind is ready. And if the quiet were no more? Would people no longer hear their consciences or their God or their fellow human beings? What is wrong with white noise, computer hum, and vacuum song? It is hard to say, except that when nature is destroyed a kind of quiet is lost. And some of our spirit is surely crushed.

Nature fills us with awe because it shows us creation and inspires us to generosity and imagination. What greater generosity can there be than the regrowth of brush from the ashes of a monstrous fire? What fertility and plenitude and growth. Flowers grow from a bloody battleground. Every day the world begins again, and we are moved with hope and the desire to create and mimic creation. If we could no longer see baby birds crying for food, if every year brought only Silent Spring, in Rachel Carson's phrase, would we be inspired to hope and create? Or would we lose our understanding of creation, and wouldn't our spirit then be crushed?

Love of nature is deep within us since we are part of nature, and since we are part of a tradition that finds nature fascinating and awe inspiring. Seasonal holidays, holidays of gratitude—it takes only the most fleeting second to remember all the trees, flowers, animals, and natural elements that fill our religious days. Easter means lilies, Palm Sunday means palm fronds, and Christmas means trees. The Jewish harvest festival of Sukkot is called the Festival of Booths, and for that holiday Jews construct small outdoor shelters to remember life lived close to nature. More and more personal spiritual experiences are held out-of-doors, more weddings and memorials and parties. Outdoor sunrise services are common on Easter morning. It is fashionable. It's pretty. It also seems that guests fit in better out-of-doors; their idiosyncrasies seem to fade with more air and light. Or maybe people are just in a better mood. Oxygen is a great mood elevator.

So if nature is so important to us, we should be able to find it in our written tradition. We can. "God created the heaven and the earth" and "God saw that it was good." The Bible begins with a statement of the earth's goodness, and almost every interpretation of the Creation carries with it a human responsibility to keep it good. One Jewish interpretation of the Creation says that since people were created last, God said to them, Take care of this earth, for none will come after you. There will be no one else to repair it if you despoil it. In our shared tradition humans have a responsibility to mind the earth.

While it is true that in the Bible mankind is given control over the natural world, that role is meant to involve conservation. The Sabbath day, or day of rest, the seventh day, is meant to be a day free of economic activity. It is a day for replenishing both human energy and natural resources. The sabbatical year, or the seventh year, is meant to be a year of replenishment. In the Bible no indentured servants can be held for more than six years; they must be released on the seventh. After six years of cultivation a field lies fallow for the seventh year. And in the jubilee year, according to Jewish tradition, after a cycle of seven sevens, property reverts to former owners, slaves are freed, debts are forgiven; the economy begins again.

These enforced periods of rest represent an early limits-to-growth philosophy. The message is, The world is precious; it is a nonexpanding resource. Treat it wisely and it will flourish. A field left fallow for one year produces better crops the following six. You will not get good work out of a servant indentured for more than six years. And a permanent slave population is more a liability than an asset. Beyond this economic wisdom, though, there is economic justice. Built into the Biblical resource system is a system of justice that ensures that workers and owners will be willing to work together to preserve resources. If there is a hope of jubilee, if there is a chance for wrongs to be righted, if there is even the glimmer of a change, then we really can work together, can't we?

The movement to preserve and sustain the environment is actually inseparable from the desire to work together toward a strong and just economy. We fight not only for clean air and clean water, but also for environmental justice. It is not good enough for the rich to have clean air and for the poor to die of black lung disease and emphysema. It is not good enough for the rich to recycle, only to put their waste treatment plants in poor and powerless neighborhoods. Environmentalism should encompass the needs of the entire economy, not just one park or one city. Some observers have suggested a new jubilee, a year of return, regrouping, and renewal. Imagine a year during which smokestacks stop, debts are forgiven, ownership is reevaluated, and the economy begins again. It is a pipe dream, perhaps, but a dream that expresses our hope for a world that is the best it can be—clean, just, and productive.

When Biblical figures controlled their environment they conserved and cherished it. God instructed the ancient Hebrews, When you do battle against a city, you may eat the fruit from your enemies' trees, but you must not cut down the trees. That would be an unnecessary—and wasteful—brutality. This instruction gave rise to the doctrine of *lo taschit*, which can be summarized as "not to destroy," but which we can call conservation. Do not destroy wantonly, the Bible says. If you need one cow for meat, do not take two. If you need two trees for wood, do not take three. If a building stands, do not destroy it. If a work is good, do not harm it. God saw the Earth and saw that it was good. Do not mindlessly ruin a beautiful work.

And everywhere, everywhere, continue God's work. A young man was surprised to see a man three times his age planting trees. "Old man," the younger one cried, "why are you planting trees? The sun is hot and you are old. You are so old, you will never live to eat the fruit of those trees. Why, who knows if you'll even see them blossom? And still you are there digging these holes. What madness." The old man looked up. "The earth wasn't bare when I arrived. Who planted the trees that I enjoyed, but some crazy old man who didn't live to seem them grow? Since the earth wasn't bare when I arrived, I will leave trees for those who follow me."

According to scriptural tradition, Adam and Eve did not arrive on a bare earth, but lived in a garden. Gardens are God's work on earth. Flowers, trees, vines, grapes, buds, and blossoms are all symbols in church and temple decoration. The medieval Christian philosopher Saint Thomas Aquinas even conceived of God as a Divine gardener, and medieval Christianity found rich symbolism and spiritual strength in monastery gardens. The monastic tradition in medieval Europe kept alive an ancient love of nature at a time when cities were squalid and the open countryside was wartorn. Within the monastery garden peace, order, and quiet reigned. Mon-

asteries were self-contained, self-sustaining units that used and conserved resources. Monks grew medicinal herbs and reflected on
man's relationship to earth and sky. One monk, Walafrid Strabo,
wrote a poem about gardening in the ninth century. He dedicated
his poem to his old teacher Grimald, the abbot of a nearby Swiss
abbey. Sometimes in his poem Walafrid dominates the earth. He
digs tangled roots, raises rectangular beds, and plants only those
plants whose usefulness justifies their presence in his garden. At
other times, though, his love of the earth is tender, personal, and
caring. He waters his seeds drop by drop, letting the water run
through his fingers so that the seeds will not be disturbed by the
rush of the water.

Ten centuries later another monk, Gregor Mendel, used his
famous garden to study God's design. Examining the flowers, one
generation after the next, he unraveled the laws of genetics, and his
conclusions still direct our study today.

Where the Bible is, there is nature and planting. Modern
Israel's proudest achievement is "making the desert bloom," planting
forests and orchards and making a once barren land fertile. It is an
agricultural achievement and an economic achievement, but it is
also a spiritual achievement. Fertility, creation, generosity, and the
promise of a new place are spiritual ideas.

What have we in the West done with our nature tradition?
We have mirrored God's goodness in gardens and done God's work
on farms. We have sought regularities and patterns, like the geneti-
cist Gregor Mendel, and we have developed a realist and naturalist
perspective in philosophy, science, and art. There is in Western
tradition a long history of landscape art.

Of all the images and styles and ideas we call Western, one
of the most instantly recognizable is the naturalism in art that is
based on perspective. The Western eye is so trained to look for

foreground and background, vanishing lines and horizons, that any other perspective doesn't look "real." We think of anything else as "primitive" and the naturalist landscape as "more advanced" because that's how the scene "really" looks. That is Western naturalism talking, the European and American fascination with the natural landscape.

Where did this Western perspective come from? Kenneth Clark, the art historian and lecturer, gives it a date: 1420. But he's hard-pressed to give it a name. It's not a science, exactly. The optical lenses that let the Dutch experiment with visions of nature come much later. This development is only partly a result of an interest in certainty. It's not meant to create physical fact, exactly. A lot of the interest in perspective was mathematical, almost purely theoretical, having little to do with the physical senses at all. Vasari, the great chronicler of his age and its artists, said that Paolo Uccello, an artist of the early 1400s, would have been a better artist if he had just opened his eyes and stopped obsessing about perspective.

> Paolo Uccello would have been the cleverest and most original genius . . . if he would have studied figures and animals as much as he studied and wasted his time over perspective, for although it is an ingenious and fine science, yet he who pursues it out of measure throws away his time, makes his manner dry, and often himself becomes solitary and strange, melancholy and poor.

Poor Uccello became delirious with perspective. His wife said he studied perspective all night, and when she would call him to bed, he would answer, "Oh, what a sweet thing this perspective is!"

Perspective is not "reality," but an invention of the Western mind, including Uccello's. It expresses ideas people in the West wanted to express. One characteristic of perspective in art is the

particular arrangement of shapes in space, some in front, some behind. The idea this expresses is time, as if you could walk through
the painting seeing the front things first, then the others later. The
viewer could progress through the painting, just as time progresses,
from Creation to the Kingdom of God.

Another characteristic of this kind of naturalist art is the
effect of light. Kenneth Clark says it is as if the sun first shone
sometime in the 1400s. If the sun is in one place, then it casts
shadows, all of which are consistent. You can tell where anything is
from its relation to the sun. That is also perspective.

One theory is that the idea of light actually came from illuminated manuscripts, whose gold-leaf decoration inspired monks to
think of new ways to show light. Or maybe the sun just began to
shine in the 1400s. Not too long after, at the end of the century and
the beginning of the next, Copernicus declared that the sun was the
center of our solar system. Whatever the origin, the use of light in
perspective painting also happens to express a very Western Judeo-
Christian idea. Just as there is one light source, there is one God,
illuminating the world from one all-knowing vantage point, sometimes in bright revelation and sometimes shadowed in ambiguity.

In other words, we paint the world, its land, its mountains,
its rivers, in the colors of our own ideas and beliefs. Naturalism
is our way of understanding nature. It combines the technique of
perspective with the belief that God is revealed in every detail of
the natural world, and were we only to look, we could grasp God's
meaning. In the nineteenth century this idea lay behind John Con-
stable's landscapes. Filled with faith in the meaning of the natural
world, the painter said, "I never saw an ugly thing in my life." This
realistic depiction of the natural world proclaimed the world good.
It also said that all people could look at and enjoy nature equally, as
long as they were familiar with the stuff of nature, with grass and

trees. Not that everyone liked naturalism. In the nineteenth century the French Count of Nieuwerkerke denounced realistic portrayals of nature as "the painting of democrats, of those who don't change their linen."

Artists have been obsessed with the Earth's power, its mystery, and, above all, its beauty. Just as we have come to define justice in natural terms, we have also come to define beauty in natural terms. Thousands of years of art and literature have celebrated the land, declared our love for it, and taught us to see rivers and forests as objects of aesthetic pleasure and meaning.

Now add one more thing. Sheep. Without these hairy creatures it would be impossible to understand the Western relationship to this Earth because, in truth, much of what we do with God's earth is own it. Sheep did not give men and women this idea of ownership; that is a long and different story. All sheep do is wander. As it turns out, that is enough.

People had lived in cooperation with sheep for millennia. Starting in the 1500s in England, however, in response to the growing wool industry throughout Europe, landowners looked to increase their flocks of sheep. Sheep were wonderfully profitable, what with their Rapunzel-like ability to turn grass into gold. The only problem was, they tended to wander. One had to enclose them, fence up the land. This enclosure movement in England displaced thousands of poor tenant farmers, whose presence was not as profitable as sheep in their landlords' estimation. For the first time in English history the human intimacy to the land was declared meaningless and easily broken. Certainly kings had had control of whole forests while peasants had no more than the rights to search for a twig or two. There had always been rich and poor. What there had never been, though, was land used for economic gain *outside of and to the exclusion of* human subsistence. Estates were enclosed. Former monastic lands were enclosed. Former common grazing lands were enclosed. The displaced fled to the cities to feed a new phenomenon: industry. And with the enclosure struggles fresh in their minds, the struggle over land and land use as clear in their minds as their conceptions of beauty, goodness, and God, English colonists left to start a New World.

BRANCHES

The North American continent was awe inspiring. It was huge. It was beautiful. Its winters were cruel beyond words. Its swamps were a hellish expanse of disease and death. Only the most enflamed visionary could see gain or conquest in the New World's forests. Many did. But many settlers thought only of survival in this astounding Eden. If any land belonged to God, thought the Pilgrims, it must be this. Here, where there were no princes, nor even landlords, the fields were not enclosed. Settlers quickly set about claiming the land, constructing towns, and otherwise re-creating the culture they knew. Still they knew that something about America was different. Blessed. An example. A city upon a hill. The citizens were careful to protect common pasture, town greens, and other common property, for they lived as communities; their fortunes were bound together. John Winthrop, the Puritan settler, wrote before landing in New England, "We must delight in each other; make others' condition our own; rejoice together, mourn together, labor and suffer together, always sharing before our eyes our commission and community in the work, as members of the same body. So shall we keep the unity of the spirit in the bond of peace."

This North American continent was different. Its people appeared to European settlers not to care about or for the land. Now we see it differently. Now we ask, is there something from this North American continent's history and people that we need to learn? A part of a speech given by Chief Seattle, translated and transcribed on the occasion of its delivery as an oration in reply to the governor of the newly organized Washington Territory in 1853, expresses many of the lessons we could learn from North America's native peoples.

> Every part of this soil is sacred in the estimation of my people. Every hillside, every valley, every plain and grove, has been hallowed by some sad or happy event in the days long vanished. Even the rocks, which seem to be dumb and dead as they swelter in the sun along the silent shore, thrill with memories of stirring events connected with the lives of my people, and the very dust upon which you now stand responds more lovingly to their footsteps than to yours, because it is rich with the blood of our ancestors. . . . At night when the streets of your cities and villages are silent and you think them deserted, they will throng with the returning hosts that once filled them and still love this beautiful land.

A prayer of the Yokuts tribe of California says, "My words are tied in one with the great mountains, with the great rocks, with the great trees."

Now we see the native peoples as embodying the special spirituality of this special place. Can we learn about caring for the earth from people who lived on this earth before us?

Can we learn from our own ancestors? Many Americans have their roots in America's agricultural past. No matter where our ancestors lived, though, we seem to have lost touch with some common and intimate knowledge of the natural world; we lack the deep connection our ancestors may have had. Fruit needs sun to ripen. When the sun is hot, the fruit becomes soft and sweet, and the season has come to breathe the sweetness and taste the soft fruit.

Nothing seems more obvious than the simple association of hot summer with strawberries and peaches. This simple natural association means nothing to most Americans. The locus of the mystery has changed. Once people asked, how does fruit ripen? Now people ask, who controls the fruit industry? There are frozen peaches, canned peaches, imported peaches, peaches anytime. The store is air-conditioned; the car is air-conditioned. Even if it is summer, what relationship is there between the hot sun and a peach, anyway? In the United States today fruit does not ripen; it spoils. Everyone knows what waiting too long looks like. It's just that no one knows what waiting looks like.

What was it that took out of American life the natural experience of eating ripe fruit? For one thing, it was the desire to make fruit more widely available, to make fruit affordable. It worked. It's just that the process had other consequences, too. Most of us will not return to growing crops, and most of us will not hunt caribou in the Alaskan wilderness. Most of us will not even jar our own watermelon pickle, and many of us will not plant a single rose. As human beings, though, we crave, we require, the intimate experience of sun and moon, sand and water, earth and earth's bounty. We need a rhythm to our world and a natural world to nourish our senses. What has happened to this connection to nature?

The sheep won. The economic use of our earth has won out over the human use of our earth. We have conquered and built and enclosed. Instead of feeding the American spirit, we have been displacing the American spirit. Profit and gain have taken precedence over beauty and goodness. There are those who claim that wealth in this world signifies God's favor. They preach greed as American theology. Greed is not a theology. It is just greed. Just as landlords once believed they would make more money on sheep, manufacturers now believe they will make more money if they pour deadly gases in the air or waste into the water.

More than that, we have turned over our village greens and common pastures. We have lost sight of our common good and our land-grant tradition. The United States of America holds its lands in common, in a trust for its people. The United States is not a collection of fiefdoms and never was. And whether or not you find its acquisition of this continent violent, unjust, or unscrupulous, the United States acquired this continent in the name of all of its people. So everyone who chooses to live here owns that history. No small settler band conquered one corner and carved out a kingdom. We hold this country in common. Our village greens need to be bigger. Our common lands must accommodate more people. We work for a common good, the cleanliness and preservation of our land.

Teddy Roosevelt said that a democracy must remain progressive or it will cease to be a democracy. Just as he saw that action was required to preserve good government, he also saw that action was required to preserve the land. Sagamore Hill, on Oyster Bay in New York, was the home of Theodore Roosevelt, the twenty-sixth president of the United States. He was an Episcopalian. Now Sagamore Hill is open to the public, so that the public can see the private Roosevelt. No matter how many visitors come, the estate is never crowded, nor dated, even under the visitors' Nikes and Reeboks. No matter where the sun is in the sky, Sagamore Hill has the honey glow of sunlight on wood, as if built for a golden age. The dining room is paneled in dark wood and is so small that more than a family, a bell, and a servant could barely fit. Yet the expanse of surrounding modern split-levels and minimalist lofts looks sad and poor compared to that dining room, windowless, at the house's core.

Roosevelt's study is at the very front of the house, and its glows mostly reddish; his wife's parlor across from it looks cooler, and small tufted chairs suggest visitors wearing long, heavy skirts. Both rooms, everywhere, have polished wood, as if the house grew in that spot of its own accord, like a tree, facing the sun and stretching its roots toward Oyster Bay. A huge tree reaches toward an upper story window, where children sneaked down, as if from one tree to another, as if stairs and branches were all one to them. There is no house better suited to summer adventures. The children's rooms upstairs are full of unexpected corners and tiny, hidden spaces, so a spy might watch his prey unsuspected.

The great room, with great windows, is full of Roosevelt's hunting trophies: bearskin rugs and animal heads. Every other trophy room everywhere is a pale copy of this one, Roosevelt's trophies representing not a life's ambition, but a love. Throughout the house, glass-fronted bookcases attest to Roosevelt's seriousness.

Of all the monuments and restorations in America, only Sagamore Hill looks like a home. Of all the theme parks and reconstructions and other tourist attractions, only Sagamore Hill seems authentic, because it expresses its owner's love of nature, and Teddy Roosevelt's love of nature became a national legacy. This love is so much a part of our vocabulary that his house feels like home. A bit refined for a Tom Sawyer, perhaps, but the water's there and the trees are there—Tom could get used to it soon enough.

At the time of Teddy Roosevelt's presidency, many prominent Episcopalians were contributing to public life in government, finance, industry, and philanthropy. The years before the First World War were optimistic years of prosperity and glamour. Not everyone in Theodore Roosevelt's crowd cared much for the rigors of camp life. Yet he had a vision of man in nature and was able to gain the necessary support to create our system of National Parks and begin the process of preserving wilderness in America.

At the time of Teddy Roosevelt's presidency, immigrants were arriving in New York. Early Jewish immigrants to the United States received a pamphlet published by the Daughters of the American Revolution and printed in Yiddish, encouraging them to leave the port city of New York and settle throughout the beautiful country. Many did. Historically, though, Jews lived in cities. For many centuries Jews were not allowed to own land.

People who live in cities can love the land; yes. But Jewish motivation to save the environment is contemporary, like the motivation of all other American groups. It is part science, part policy, part conscience, and part hope. The threat of global warming, with its concomitant melting of the polar ice caps, rise in sea level, and change in global atmosphere, is a threat to which we are only now awakening. The destruction of the rainforest, and with it the destruction of countless plants containing medicinal compounds yet to be fully discovered, is happening now. Some of the motivation behind environmentalism is scientific; some is economic. As nonrenewable resources like coal and oil dwindle, we wonder, what would life be like in a world with less energy? What would life be like in a world where the depleted ozone layer makes skin cancer a commonplace? What would life be like in a browner, grayer, drier, sludgier world?

The environmental movement represents a chance for all groups to participate fully and unreservedly in America's work as equals and as partners. For while some groups may have owned more land, and some may have farmed more land, when it comes to repairing the earth, all American nonnative groups are novices. In America the children of citydwellers and the children of farmers go hiking together.

The religious community supports environmental protection because when people nurture and care for the environment, they nurture and care for each other. Scientists can explain the threats to Americans' physical health. Environmental lobbyists can explain the threats to particular species or ecosystems. But the religious community can explain American values: we value our nature tradition and our tradition of intervening to care for our earth. When we care for our earth we are more human. We remember who we are, our brevity, our smallness, our creative urge, our sensual pleasure. Without these, our spirit is crushed.

A NEW LEAF

Imagine an outsider seeing our world from a distance. Many environmentalists do this. Sometimes, as among religious groups, such as the National Religious Partnership for the Environment, that outside viewer is God. Sometimes people speak of our children and our children's children, far into the future. Sometimes people speak of Native Americans or their own ancestors and wonder what they would say about our care of the environment today. These invisible partners give us a sense of responsibility to something larger than ourselves. They place us in an unending chain. They give us, here, now, a sense of common purpose. So the environmentalist metaphor "spaceship Earth" evokes an outside viewer who sees us all on this ship together. The unnamed outside viewer makes a judgment: are we destroying something beautiful, or are we caring for it and letting it flourish? This outside viewer gives us a moral challenge. Future generations might say of us, "Did they leave us some spiritual peace, or did they erase all traces of nature and our part in it?"

While this moral guideline sounds good, it is a tough row to hoe. First of all, does this absent other really see where I leave my empty Snapple bottle? If the people walking all around me don't seem to care, how do I know future generations, or the native American legacy, or even God cares? Sure, maybe some abstract principle is important for understanding something big and important, like the ozone layer, but why must I give up my beachfront property to allow for the preservation of wetlands, for the sake of something so distant? The future, the past, outer space—it is all so far away.

Too often, in an attempt to make environmental issues more pressing and personal, advocates for the environment link moral demands and political demands. We're not doing this for some outside other, they say. No, it's Us against Them. Either you're With Us or you're Against Us. Choose sides. And nature, mind you, is on Our Side. Now, the political role of nature is very old. Nature has worn a Jacobin's bonnet, a democrat's coonskin cap, and a fascist's brown shirt. Nature has hunted bear with Teddy Roosevelt and studied global warming with Al Gore. But the demand "Do this because we say so" is no easier than the demand "Do this because others are watching." Both are tough rows to hoe. After all, who is going to tie up those papers for recycling? Who is going to join the carpool and install new water-saving attachments to my toilet? Is Teddy Roosevelt going to wash out my empty bottles?

So our shared tradition brings to the environmental table two indispensable tools: moral outrage and common decency. These capacities are to be found within and not without. They belong to no one political party. They belong to every individual and can be used individually. They are our very own Judeo-Christian birthright, and they give voice to the best within us.

Moral outrage is the feeling that makes you yell, "This is not right!" More than a sense of right and wrong, it is the willingness to publicly proclaim one's sense of right and wrong, as well as to publicly act on it. Dissatisfaction can be found anywhere. What culture or society has been devoid of malcontents, grumps, or those disappointed by life? Moral outrage is not just dissatisfaction. Greek soothsayers and Roman augurs foretold ill fortune and even cursed a world gone awry. But moral outrage is not just a reading of the stars. Moral outrage says, "This is not right. *Do otherwise.*" Underlying the feeling of outrage is the belief that the world can be changed and we can change it. Greek soothsayers did not believe they could change the course of history. But we do believe it.

Moral outrage says, "The world is not good enough, *and we can do better.*"

When Moses said to Pharaoh, "Let my people go," he was saying, "This is wrong, and we will do otherwise." When Jesus argued against the defilers of the temple, he was saying, "This is wrong, and we will do otherwise. We will change history armed only with our own sense of right and wrong. Ours is the tradition of the prophets, who foresaw not only destruction, but a new, peaceable kingdom." Moral outrage has driven us toward a better, more just world because in our tradition one person can say, "This is not right."

The great thing about moral outrage is that it knows no time clock, no moment, and no statute of limitations. It owes nothing to the past and looks only to the future. For thousands of years human beings enslaved one another, for hundreds of years on this continent. But then we said, "This will not stand," and the moral outrage over slavery became a historical force. It does not matter if we have dirtied our land, razed forests, cut gashes into the earth, and strip-mined in the most violent way. What matters is that we can, at any time, say, "This will not stand. This is not right, and we will do otherwise." There is no deadline on morality. We can say it now and start a better world tomorrow.

Chief Seattle can give us sadness. He can give us responsibility or awareness. Only our own tradition can give us the righteous anger that fuels change. Pollution is not right. As long as you believe that, you must be angry about it. You must be angry about each soda can discarded on the sidewalk. You must be outraged at the destruction of the rainforest, incensed at industrial greed, and furious over individual waste. It is not right, and now we are saying we will do otherwise.

Although the story of Noah and the Flood seems to speak to

our concerns about the earth, Noah is not a hero, precisely for his lack of outrage. In fact, Noah's indifference so enraged rabbis of later generations that rabbinic authors created a dialogue that they believed should have been included in the biblical text: After the flood was over and Noah had released all the animals, he and his family stood on dry ground. Surveying the devastation, Noah asked, "God, how could you have done this? How could you have allowed all of humanity to be swept away by this flood?"

God thundered back, "Fool! I described at length what I planned to do before the flood so that you might ask mercy for the world. But as soon as you heard that you would be safe in the ark, the evil of the world did not touch your heart. You built the ark and saved yourself. Now that the world has been destroyed, you ask questions and offer pleas? Where was your compassion and pity when it could have made a difference? . . . Noah, you are too late!"

AS POWERFUL AS MORAL OUTRAGE IS, OUR MOST powerful tool is really common decency. Common decency is common in the sense that it is simple, and common in the sense that it is universal. It is as simple as do unto others what you would have others do unto you. Treat others—animals, the earth, trees, property —with respect. It is a sad and amazing time in America that we need to define common decency. We must make a case for it, argue our case and advertise it. Who would have guessed thirty years ago that the simplest ideas of caring for our people, caring for our environment, and caring for our own humanity would be attacked by a right wing so rabid it would slash the very land on which it stands? But there it is. And here we are, defending the core of our very culture, common decency.

In our shared tradition common decency means gentleness. Christians who strive to walk in the steps of Jesus strive to be gentle and forgiving, to turn the other cheek. The life of Jesus as it is recounted in the Gospels is full of images of mildness: the Madonna and Child, Jesus the healer, Jesus the teacher. It is impossible to imagine Jesus screaming, hurling epithets, or even expressing thoughts of bitterness or hostility. That is not what He is about. While the histories of all the countries of the world have certainly consisted at one time or another of atrocity and rage, our ideal of common decency is an ideal of gentleness toward others.

Common decency also means respect for privacy, not only physical privacy, but the privacy of thought, feeling, and emotion. The Jewish text known as *Sayings of the Fathers* cautions the reader: a decent person does not approach a grieving person in the instant of his grief but waits for an opportune moment. A decent person does not trample the joy of another. So, tradition has it that all brides are beautiful—to say otherwise would crush someone's private joy. And, as the saying goes, in the house of a hanged man one doesn't talk about rope. A decent person does not remind someone of his or her private sorrow.

Gentleness and respect for privacy are two aspects of restraint. Common decency, in our tradition, means restraint. We rein in our emotions and our desires, putting them second to what is truly human in us, thought and belief. The Biblical tradition shows one figure after another sacrificing his or her love or fear or desire in the name of a common good. The great Jewish heroine Esther jeopardizes her comfort as queen in order to save her people.

Our ideal, in other words, is a thoughtful, gentle person who leaves wide spaces between himself or herself and other people's feelings. We consider untrammeled emotion childlike. Or mad. Common decency, in our world, is not mad, but rational, linking cause and effect, doer and deed. It is not decent for a man to go home and beat his wife and child because he did not win the lottery; it is violent, unthinking, and irrational. It is not decent for a person to vote to close down halfway houses and drug treatment centers because he suspects that the money he pays in taxes is what's preventing him from becoming rich; that is violent, unthinking, and irrational. Any person who, out of anger and frustration, votes to end programs to feed the poor has lost his or her sense of common decency.

Likewise, a person who burns or destroys the earth has lost his or her sense of common decency. It is common decency, that ideal of gentleness, privacy, and rationality, that tells us not to litter, not to destroy property, and to treat the Earth with care and sensitivity.

In the presence of death we feel fear and uncertainty. We are hushed and restrained. Even in the presence of the death of animals we feel awe and restraint. The American observer Garrison Keillor, commenting on the slaughter of cattle, remarked that the youngest child is taught quiet and restraint on this subject. No one laughs when they slaughter a steer. Or, at least, no decent person does. Jewish kosher laws have long been exacting and explicit about the method of slaughter. Many commentators interpret this as sensitivity toward the suffering of animals who have no choice and less understanding. At the same time, these laws tell us something about common decency. For centuries only one ritual slaughterer practiced his trade in each town, and he had to be rigorously certified. That, commentators say, is so that only one person trafficked in death. Dealing in death hardens people, and were too many people to become hardened to death, we would all lose our hush, our restraint —our awe.

Now think about the extinction of species. It happens; it is part of nature. The evolutionary biologist Stephen Jay Gould even pointed out that as an evolutionary biologist, he could hardly argue against the extinction of species. But as we let species become extinct without remark or remorse, aren't we becoming hardened to death? Aren't we replacing awe with exploitation, and in doing so becoming less decent ourselves?

We were not the first here; it cannot be that we were meant to be the last.

VI

Tending Fields

There is violence where there should be peace.

In this story, a woman tries to quell the violence of those close to her.

Blessed are the peacemakers. But why did it fall to Elizabeth, again, to avert war? Since her marriage to Denis, King of Portugal, when she was twelve years old, she had led an exemplary life, a life of devotion, prayer, charity. A life of discipline. She founded a hospital, an orphanage, a house for women. Yet the harder she tried, the more people admired her. The more they admired her, the more reckless they were themselves. Try as she might to make order in her world, she found herself surrounded by violence, hostility, and disagreement. It seemed that the well of violence was never ending. Her husband. Her son, Alfonso. It was as if the world were mad with weapons. Twice Alfonso raised armies against her husband, the king. Both times Elizabeth rode out onto the field between the two opposing forces to reconcile them. Why was her son so rebellious? And why did her husband leave her the job of peacemaker? She stopped a war between Ferdinand II of Castile and his cousin and another war between that prince and her brother, James II of Aragon. Surely that was enough. It was so thankless. It was so dangerous and frightening, the job of emptying battlefields.

And that is why, after her husband's long illness and death, she wanted to retire to a convent. At the convent of Poor Clares, which she had founded at Coimbra, life would be orderly. Prayers would not be interrupted by knights bursting upon the scene brandishing swords. Meals would not be punctuated by threats and the hostile flash of reds and golds and black leather. The laughter would not be so loud and insinuating, and the sorrow of distance would not seem so cold. But the people wouldn't let her go to the convent. They said they needed her help. They said her gifts of peacemaking were needed. So she didn't live in the convent, but near the convent. And she continued her errands of reconciliation.

Why wouldn't anyone else follow her path? If they loved her, why didn't *they make peace? Didn't they know that that one last errand of reconciliation would kill her at sixty-five, when the heat of journey was unbearable? Saint Elizabeth of Portugal died in 1336. She died trying to put sanity back in her world. It's not only those who live by the sword who die by the sword; war kills peacemakers, too.*

꙰

NO RELIGION WILL ARGUE THAT THE WORLD IS NOT full of violence and pain. It is. Whether this is because of the fall from grace or the incompleteness of God's work, whether violence is temporary and aberrant or basic to life's design, it is part of human history. Now, religions preach war and religions preach peace, but religions mostly preach peace. Our traditions value peace and share a vision of America as a refuge of peace. Why do we dare dream of peace in a violent world? How do we dare speak the words when every day the newspapers tell of the very opposite: war, strife, violence, death? And why do we claim this hope for America, of all places, this wild, gun-ridden country where children no longer die of polio, but of gunshot wounds? Let us now think for a few moments about peace. The thought almost begins with a deep breath.

A NASTY, BRUTISH LIFE

Religions agree on the necessity of peace because it is a fundamental prerequisite to all social life, all thought, and all achievement. Whatever else you might consider the Ten Commandments, first and last, taken at simple face value, they are a prescription for maintaining social order. Thou shalt not kill. The observation is simple and thousands of years old: when the killing starts, civilization ends. It is no coincidence that the Bible bids us beat our "swords into plowshares" and our "spears into pruning hooks"; when people are busy killing one another, they are not sowing and reaping. They are neither feeding themselves nor planning for the future. War eats up resources, including the most valuable ones, human lives. Human beings who die in battle are not producing food, producing children, composing music, curing disease. Violence is wasteful. Can a social order be built on bloodshed and conquest? Yes, of course. We do not, however, consider that a good world. That is not our ideal for human life.

First, violence conflicts with our sense of equality, our brother- and sisterhood under God. The Bible's first murder is one brother killing another brother; God asks Cain, "Where is your brother?" In other words, each time a man is killed, we lose a brother. Our common humanity is lessened.

Violence is inconsistent with our special status, godlike, created in God's image. We are halfway between the angels and the animals in Judeo-Christian tradition, and violence and killing is a base and animal part of us. When the seventeenth-century political philosopher Thomas Hobbes wanted to describe the tendency to violence and selfishness he said, *"Homo homini lupus,"* or "Man is as a wolf unto other men."

Violence is inconsistent with our emphasis on control and rational thought. It is inconsistent with our shared injunction to treat others as you want to be treated. It is inconsistent with our future-oriented outlook. We look back at prolonged periods of warfare as grim, tragic times. The period in Western Europe between the years 500 and 1000 in the Common Era were years of war, plunder, and conquest. While we may one day return to a world of walled enclosures, wandering beggars, and private armies, we fear that as a dark and frightening age.

On the other hand, we associate peace with prosperity. When the medieval wars ended, food production increased, trade flourished. Peace is so fundamental to social order that organized religion can claim its own benefits: in peace people build houses of worship, study texts, get married, educate their young, and give thanks.

Peace is a fundamental prerequisite to everything, including more peace. Violence spirals downward, creating more and more violence. Even if we had no other values or ideas to use to condemn violence, this downward spiral alone would be enough to make us sick at the thought of hostility and physical harm. The observation that violence begets more violence is deeply ingrained in our tradition. We know that children who are beaten or who witness their parents beating one another are more likely to grow up to beat their own children or spouses.

Jewish culture has an ideal of *bayit shalom,* or peace in the home, and over many centuries Judaism has developed models of the ideal father, mother, and child. Yet the story of the Sabbath spirit contains a sad recognition that these ideals are difficult to achieve. The Sabbath, especially, is supposed to be a time of calm and rest; the Sabbath is supposed to bring peace, for on the seventh day of Creation God rested. But one story says that on each Sabbath a spirit visits each household. Where there is peace the spirit says, "So shall it be next week," and the household is rewarded with peace the following week. Where there is hostility and fighting, however, the spirit also says, "So shall it be next week," and violence simply begets more violence.

Outside the household, too, bloodshed brings more bloodshed. On one of his explorations in North America the explorer Alvar Núñez Cabeza de Vaca encountered a situation that struck him as unspeakably tragic. One Native American group was at war with its neighbors. The fighting alone was regrettable, but not unusual and no different from the situation in Europe that Cabeza de Vaca had left. What struck him as tragic was that as a result of this

conflict one group was killing all of its own female children. When
he asked them why, they explained that since they were at war with
their neighbors, they could not give their women to the other tribe's
men in marriage, as they usually did. Since they considered marriage
among members of their own tribe as a form of incest, they had no
use for their female children and had to be rid of them. Not only
does external conflict often breed internal conflict, as Cabeza de
Vaca saw, but often those escalated conflicts kill innocents—peacemakers, bystanders, or true innocents, children.

Catholics believe that abortion is the murder of innocents.
Catholics believe that life begins at conception, and just as God
placed Jesus in Mary's womb, so God intends for each child conceived in each womb to live, for it was His will that placed it there.
Human beings, in this view, do not have the power or the right to
determine life and death; only God can give life or take life. Just as
Jesus said, "Let the children approach me, the Kingdom of Heaven
is theirs, too," Catholicism reserves a special place for children. The
murder of children, who cannot defend themselves either by flesh
or by spirit, is horrific.

At the same time, the tragedy for Catholics is compounded
when one violence begets another, and the violence of abortion
results in violence at or around abortion clinics. Here, again, we see
the downward spiral of death after death, violence after violence.
Protesters who express their views are understandable; protesters
who kill doctors who perform abortions or protesters who bomb or
shoot into abortion clinics are no different from any other murderers. The murderer thinks he is carrying out God's will. But only God
has the power to take life.

What if the victim is not innocent? What if we use the words
retribution and *justice?* In fact there are many words to describe the
cycle of killing and more killing. There is *vengeance, revenge* and *ven-*

detta, blood feud. There is *execution.* Once the governor of Kentucky had several women awaiting execution on death row in his prisons. They had all been convicted of murdering a husband. They had not killed an innocent person. After suffering years of torment and beatings these women had responded by turning against their tormentors and murdering them. There these women sat in the prisons in Kentucky, awaiting the ultimate punishment and sewing a quilt, constructing the pattern of their lives into a tangible form that would outlive them. The governor of Kentucky asked himself, when will this cycle of killing end? Is it up to me now to kill these women? What will be the result of these deaths? Will another generation grow up with something or someone to kill? He pardoned the women because he believed that they had more to give the world than as simply the weavers of a pattern of violence that would outlive them. Should the punishment, after all, be hundreds of years longer than the crime?

Much is made of the Biblical statement "eye for eye, tooth for tooth." For many people it has come to represent revenge, as if it demanded a minimum of an eye for an eye. There is another way to understand this statement. It is a statement of justice, demanding a maximum, not a minimum sentence—no more than a punishment that fits the crime, our Biblical ancestors said. Would you kill a man for knocking out your tooth? This is a statement about equivalencies, not revenge. So talmudic rabbis extended the meaning of the *lex talionis* (the law of retaliation equivalent to the crime) or "eye for an eye" law from Deuteronomy, by requiring financial compensation for loss of income, medical damages, damages for shame, physical or emotional pain, or suffering. Murder presents a problem. What is the equivalent of a human life? Is it a life in return? Or is that just another step in the downward spiral of one death after another?

We interpret our shared religious tradition as speaking against the death penalty. It is not the right of governments to take the lives of its citizens, even citizens accused and convicted of killing others. For some of us condemning someone to death simply goes beyond the human sphere; only God can take a life. But even for those of us who feel that we are charged with this kind of decision, capital punishment perverts our core values. Do we love justice? Execution is so final that no mistake can be corrected, no new evidence can come to light, and innocent people can be killed. Do we love the equality of all of God's creatures? Capital punishment is used selectively depending on the race of the killer and the victim.

In our society the equivalent of a life is a life spent without freedom. We may still hope that the punishment will suit the crime, but taking a life is cruel, and it is not our goal to be cruel, only fair. Do we love peace? The death penalty does not deter violence. The rates of capital crime have not declined in states where the death penalty has been reinstated. What is more, capital punishment teaches that murder is sometimes justified. In no way does it diminish violence or get to the bottom of it.

Or maybe we should reexamine our goals. Is it really one of the goals of our country *to create murderers* and then dispense with them in elaborate ways? In most states the corrections budget is higher than the budget for education. Why? Why do we need so many people behind bars? We know who is at risk of becoming the next generation of criminals. Why not spend our resources compassionately on education rather than punitively on methods of revenge? So many of our young black men spend time in prison that for many minority children prison is just another institution, like school or the emergency ward of a hospital. The day the death penalty becomes routine is the day we lose our humanity and give in to the worst in our natures.

We know that many Americans support the death penalty. That does not make it right. We know that people feel fear and hatred, despair and a longing for revenge. We know that there is widespread disenchantment and a feeling that the victims of crime are forgotten by the system. Yet we do not want Americans to forget their values: justice, equality, compassion, peace. Yes, values. We are constructing a nation, a grand experiment in idealism. Who are we if we abandon our ideals?

THE PEACEABLE KINGDOM
In 1834 Edward Hicks painted a picture that he called *The Peaceable Kingdom* and that spoke directly to his ideal for the new nation in North America. In the foreground are animals illustrating a verse from Isaiah, the Biblical image of the peaceable kingdom:

> The wolf also shall dwell with the lamb, and
> The leopard shall lie down with the kid; and
> the calf and the young lion and the fatling together;
> and a little child shall lead them.

The background of the picture, though, depicts a very human scene that explicitly and unmistakably refers to the United States. Native Americans look at some cloth displayed by colonials, as if engaged in trade. Standing with arms outstretched is William Penn. In the distance a river flows into the wilderness and into the future. This painting so clearly ties the United States to Isaiah's Biblical vision of peace that it is worth considering at some length. Why did the early settlers believe that the Bible foretold that the United States would be a peaceful haven?

Isaiah's description of the animals of the peaceable kindom clearly describes an end to predatory behavior. The predator lies with his prey, and there is an end to hunter and hunted. In fact, throughout the Bible, animals of prey do not find favor in God's eyes. People sacrifice only peaceful animals, and when sacrifices end, it is only peaceful animals that serve as positive images. Jewish lore says that one can see that God favors peace because the Bible does not praise falcons or hawks, but only doves and pigeons. The early American reflecting on Isaiah and on Hicks's painting would have found special meaning in this image, and in the lion in the painting, for the lion was one of the symbols of England and an unmistakable symbol of royalty. Aristocrats were predators in Europe, both literally because they hunted and figuratively because they demanded land and obedience from their inferiors. In America, where there was no royalty, the idea was that no rich would prey upon the poor. No royalty would threaten the peace of the common folk, the way they did in Europe. Drawn into this vision of peace, then, is the inherent equality of all those who would come to the shores of the New World.

According to the prophet Isaiah, righteousness and good government are elements of that promised time when all strife will end and joy will reign. Hicks drew into his painting literal governors to show righteous government. Thomas Paine, one of many new Americans writing about their government, wrote that the new wilderness of North America should have a suitable new righteous government, that Nature should inspire them to begin again and leave off not only Europe's inequalities, but its injustices.

In prophesying that the world must start anew, cities razed and empires fallen, before true peace will come, Isaiah also refers to a wilderness setting. Surely the North American wilderness fulfilled the prophesy for the early Americans. Hicks's wilderness is not overly wild, but it clearly looks different from the European port cities most colonists left behind. In his painting the trees form protective canopies, the river stretches into the future, and the promontories are stages for scenes of America as a haven of peace. One image is trade. Trade can be carried on only in peace. None of Hicks's figures carries weapons; one Indian has even brought a peace pipe. So trade, economic activity, would be the future of this new country and its road to peaceful settlement.

Another meaning of *The Peaceable Kingdom* would have been clear to the painter and his audience: they would recognize the young child who leads the animals as Jesus, called Prince of Peace, whose coming, Christians believed, was foretold in Isaiah. The message is that the United States would be a land without violence because it would be a religious land. That meant, for the early settlers, a Christian land, or, more specifically, a Protestant land. Religion and trade, an end to aristocratic domination, and a benevolent wilderness all made America look promising to Edward Hicks and his audience.

But the United States today is not a peaceful haven. In fact, it is a country of extreme violence, both physical and psychological. The United States is almost a perfect example of predatory behavior, made up only of hunters and hunted. Our national symbol is not the turkey, as Benjamin Franklin proposed, but a predator: the eagle. Our businessmen swim with sharks; readers can enjoy books about women who run with wolves; daily life is a rat race in a dog-eat-dog world. There are those who would look to Hicks for their solutions, hoping that with enough free markets and enough Protestantism the United States would once again look the way it did when Edward Hicks painted it in 1834. The problem is, Edward Hicks painted an ideal, not a country. The United States never really resembled Isaiah's peaceable kingdom. The reality of the United States has long been violence.

Hicks's image of cooperation between white settlers and Native Americans was an illusion. Sometimes a little at a time and sometimes wholesale, settlers stole Indian land and displaced the indigenous population. Long before the great Indian wars that led to the conquering of the West in the 1870s, long before Custer and Sitting Bull, as early as 1841, observer George Catlin made a plea on behalf of the natives of this continent. The United States was violent and observers like Catlin knew it. "It is a sad and melancholy truth to contemplate," he wrote, "that all the numerous tribes who inhabited our vast Atlantic States *have not* fled to the West;—that they are not to be found here—that they have been blasted by the fire which has passed over them—have sunk into their graves, and everything but their names travelled into oblivion."

What is more, much of the new country was built on the violence of slavery and the African slave trade. Many of us have ancestors who were in other countries on other continents when Americans were engaged in the bloody business of buying and selling human beings, abusing and degrading them, and denying their humanity. And yet the legacy of slavery is our legacy. Each time we pass the rolling hills that once were the settings of plantation life, each time we praise our textile industry or condemn our tobacco conglomerates, we acknowledge the wealth built on slave labor. The industry of those Northern cities that welcomed our ancestors grew as a result of the Civil War. Irish Catholics immigrated to fight in Union armies. We are in this American history together, inextricably bound. You may not recognize your own grandfather among Edward Hicks's American gentlemen, but he is there.

The violence of slavery became another violence, that of the Civil War. The violence of our war for independence became the violence of tax rebellions and secessionist skirmishes. The violence of industrial growth, with its tuberculosis and black lung disease, starvation wages and real starvation, became the violence of union building and strikebreaking. Even Hicks's image of trade as economic cooperation was more a hope than a reality. The economic history of the United States has a large element of violence within it.

The Catholic Church in America recognized the violence and ill treatment officially as early as 1917 when a General Conference of Catholics, representing 68 dioceses and 27 national Catholic organizations, created the National Catholic War Council. This council continued to function in peacetime, and in 1919 its Administrative Committee of Bishops produced the document "Social Reconstruction: A General Review of the Problems and Surveys of Remedies," a clear demand for fair wages and fair treatment of workers. Many of their recommendations actually became New Deal policy. The War Council ultimately became the National Catholic Welfare Conference, an effective national organization designed to counter the ravages of industrial life.

For with industry came poverty, and the United States is not the land of equals imagined by idealists two hundred years ago. The violence of poverty breeds the violence of domestic abuse, alcoholism, theft, and sheer anger and frustration. This was true of the United States one hundred years ago, fifty years ago, and it is still true today. Not only does the United States have a violent history on a grand scale, but the American people have been a belligerent lot individually.

The search for self-reliance and freedom from government intrusion have sometimes fostered feelings of violence and hatred as noted by Richard E. Nicholls in the *New York Times*. He wrote about Frederick Remington, the painter of the mythic West, who hated "Jews, Injuns, Chinamen, Italians, Huns—the rubbish of the Earth I hate." Remington's response? "I've got some Winchesters and when the massacring begins, I can get my share of 'em." The cattleman Granville Stuart led a vigilante group called "Stuart's

Stranglers" to seize and kill possibly several dozen people they believed to be horse and cattle thieves, on no authority but their own.

Americans value independence and teach their children independence. This is not because somewhere in Washington there are documents called the Declaration of Independence or the Emancipation Proclamation, but because so many of America's people have moved from place to place seeking more control over their own lives. For every cowpoke and speculator in our past, there are a dozen suburbanites who wanted more room between them and the people next door. No self-respecting American parent specifically tries to create another Billy the Kid or Jesse James, but the spirit of lawless independence is an American spirit. No playground and no nursery school today tolerates fistfighting, for example. When one child hits another child, parents or teachers pull them away and reprimand them both. At the same time, competition and the assertion of individual will are often rewarded. For instance, if a child on the playground is running up the slide, preventing others from sliding down, he will not be reprimanded—unless another child complains. Abstract rules take second place to the assertion of will. One parent sees his child running up the slide as using the equipment in an individual, creative way and "winning" at the competition of asserting his rights over the rights of others.

In corners and cultures far removed from the Wild West, vigilantes and gunslingers, neighborhood bullies have had great success. Alfred Kazin, the literary critic, wrote in his memoirs of his boyhood in a Jewish neighborhood in Brooklyn that he was tyrannized by neighborhood know-it-alls. On one occasion he was beaten up by a kid who jeered, "You haven't read any Ezra Pound, have you? If you're so smart, how come you don't know Ezra Pound?" Bullies get their comeuppance; their victims, not they, become famous literary critics. Yet the bully is as American as barbecue and Memorial Day.

Americans conceive of leadership as asserting one's will; the Japanese, in contrast, think of leadership as developing consensus. One little American boy in the 1950s found a best friend in kindergarten. This best friend, though, was more boss than companion. Whatever the friend said, the boy did. Teachers and parents alike clucked their tongues in dismay. They feared that the boy was, of all things, a follower. No leadership potential. The bossy friend was about to move away, and all the adults feared that the little follower would fall to pieces. Instead of falling to pieces, the boy simply went about his business succeeding in school. It was the bossy friend, dependent on a follower, who fell to pieces. The little boy went on to become a corporate vice president trusted with sensitive negotiations with the Japanese. Is it possible that American parents would be wise to start teaching something other than the assertion of individual will? Edward Hicks painted groups in accord; the American reality has been individuals in conflict.

There is another sad truth about America, the not so peaceable kingdom. In Hicks's painting the people carry no arms. In the real America the right to bear arms is written into the Constitution. Few countries have this legal provision. England does not. What are we to make of it? The Bible says our swords shall be plowshares and our spears pruning hooks, and the American Constitution calls for a musket beside every plow and a Bowie knife under each pillow. In one way this is the American insistence on equality: in Europe aristocrats were the warrior class, and American law reaffirms that on the new continent there would be no warrior class. In another way, it is an anachronism.

Technology has outstripped our ability to adapt to it. This is called culture lag. Why do we need guns? Few people now hunt for their own supper. Fewer people need raise a warning shot to alert neighbors; today there are telephones. Most important, the technology of weaponry is so different from that two hundred years ago that the Founding Fathers would not recognize it. It is hard to imagine an accidental death due to musket fire. It took so long to load a musket, and such deliberate effort to load the shot and the powder, that outside of mistaken identity or a hunting accident, it would be nearly impossible. Imagine the British troops in their red coats kneeling to reload during the American War for Independence. It took a minute to reload. A minute is a long time, long enough for a child mistaken as an intruder to shout, "Wait, it's me, don't shoot." Or to run. Today's guns are fast, small, light. Our houses are closer together. Our factories are faster. It's hard to understand what the right to bear arms means in this America. Does it mean the right to atomic weapons? Does it mean the right to make weapons that are faster and more lethal than those used by the police? Does it mean the right for children to find a gun in a desk and try it out?

Marian Wright Edelman, president of the Children's Defense Fund, has called the widespread death of children by gunfire "morally unthinkable." Gunfire is the second leading cause of death among Americans aged ten to nineteen. (The leading cause is accidents, usually car accidents.) We have conquered disease. We have banished starvation. It is guns that are killing our children. In 1993 5,751 people under the age of twenty died of gunshot wounds. Of those children 116 were under five years old. Does this make sense? If equal numbers of children died of polio, we would redouble our efforts at vaccinating children. We demand by law all kinds of safety precautions in automobiles, including child car seats and seat belts. What are we doing to keep children from being shot? Ms. Edelman has said, "What will it take for parents and religious, community, and political leaders to stand up and say enough?"

We are saying enough. The widespread accessibility of lethal weapons in America has become inconsistent with our hope to make America a safe haven. It has become inconsistent with our hopes for democracy. Everyone knows this classic example of the limit on democratic freedoms: the right to free speech does not imply the right to shout "Fire!" in a crowded movie theater. Freedom does not mean the freedom to endanger others. The widespread availability of weapons in this country is endangering people. The right to bear arms does not imply the right to hunt pheasant in Midtown Manhattan with a machine gun.

Perhaps violence has always been a homegrown American product. Perhaps the bully is an American character. Perhaps knife fights and fistfights have always been part of school. Must we make fighting a matter of life and death? Must we arm our children and make their fight to survive so bloody that simply giving them life is drafting them into a terrifying war?

Eighteen-year-olds, and youth even younger, have actually carried weapons into war. Teenagers are strong, often reckless, sometimes idealistic and eager to defend ideas of honor. Youth and violence have a long association. During the Middle Ages the idea of honor, chivalry, and loyalty dominated the lives of many young men. Then, as now, a town's worst fear was a group of armed young men with no foreign land to conquer. Young soldiers with no war to fight have a tendency to find their own wars. During the nineteenth century German university students revived the fight for honor by fighting bloody, but highly stylized duels. The goal was a magnificent dueling scar to symbolize one's bravery. Often, however, students died pointlessly, proving nothing but their ability to be influenced by their peers. The German dueling societies taught barbarism and inhumanity. Did they also satisfy a teenage need for excitement or even violence? Social scientist William McAuliffe, an expert on drug addiction, had a novel theory. He argued that no drug program replaced the self-destructive thrill of illegal drug use. He suggested that violent and potentially dangerous activities such as racing cars or skydiving might actually draw young people from the lure of drugs whereas basketball cannot.

All of these elements—the youth, the danger, the self-destructive tendencies, the need for honor, the lack of other realms of conquest—contribute to gang wars in the United States. Gang members fight over drugs, but they also fight over territory and that elusive thing "honor." Honor means pride. In a world where there is precious little to feel proud of, gangs supply an answer. In the face of this, religions teach humility. Don't be proud, be humble. In the age-old conflict between the red and the black, or the army and the clergy, the clergy have preached peace and humility. Pride and arrogance lead to suffering; only in humility can one approach God. When the self-important braggard is not an object of reproach, he is the butt of jokes and lessons. One object lesson concerned Henry Kissinger, a man whose overweening pride in his achievements has struck many people as inappropriate. He traveled all over the world, the story went, trying to have a suit made for him from a special bolt of cloth. The finest tailors in London, Hong Kong, and Milan all said they couldn't possibly do it—not enough cloth. Finally a tailor in Tel Aviv agreed. He made Kissinger a coat, a vest, two pairs of pants, and a raincoat liner. Shocked, Kissinger said, "How did you do it? The others all said it was impossible." The tailor was unimpressed. "Around here we don't think you're such a big man."

Humility and *peace* may be the legitimate words of the clergy. The problem is that in a world where gang members shoot and hit innocent children, those words sound distant, reproachful, and unrealistic. It sounds as if members of the clergy do not recognize that the streets are hard. Small children say, "I need a gun to protect myself. Why will God protect me when he didn't protect my friend who was shot last year?" Humility is a strange lesson to learn when all around you advertisements say you have failed: you are not sexy enough, not tough enough, not rich enough, not attractive enough, not thin enough. And then the clergy directs one more criticism your way: you are not humble enough.

Americans need something that is neither pride nor humility. Honor and pride are too quick to anger. Humility is too quick to scrape and shuffle. Let's call our middle ground "courage." Imagine living in a country of really courageous people. If you had a beef with someone, you would let him know. How many times have you just avoided someone because you were angry with him? How many times did you wish you had the courage to say what you felt? Imagine if everyone did that. There might be so many more arguments. Yet there might be so many fewer guns. Day after day the newspapers print stories of so-called disgruntled workers who return to their workplace with a gun. We don't think they should have the guns. We don't think they should need guns. Gang members with the courage to face other gang members would look different. Children with the courage to walk to school would look different. Can we change an American tradition of violence into an American tradition of courage? How can we create truly courageous people?

ADAM OR EVE ALONE

If our shared religious tradition preached peace solely for the sake of social order and discipline, we could stop here. We could say control the guns, create youth programs, and reduce the number of children in poverty. All of these steps would curb violence. Then we could even suggest a secondary approach—reduce the modeling of violent behavior, raise awareness about domestic abuse, and end capital punishment. These strategies would create a more peaceful society.

Our shared religious tradition, though, teaches peace for other reasons beyond encouraging the constructing of a peaceable kingdom or the forging of some specific society. Religions all over the world, in societies drastically different from our own, all teach the same lesson—peace. We would like to forget the violence in our own pasts, the violence committed in the name of our own religions. We would rather focus on examples of decency and achievement. There is both good and bad, after all. Forgetfulness, though, is unconvincing. Can you really disinherit pieces of your own past? Groucho Marx, in the college comedy *Horsefeathers*, tries to impress a companion. "I'm Professor Wagstaff of Huxley College," he says, whipping out an imaginary business card. His companion is unimpressed. "That means nothing to me." So Groucho whips out an alternative imaginary card. "I'm Professor Huxley of Wagstaff College." His companion is even less impressed the second time. "You didn't stay at the other college very long." Changing your past to make a good impression, as Groucho tried, seldom works.

One reason we cannot forget the violence associated with religion is that is has been of massive historical significance. The Crusades, begun at the urging of Pope Urban X in 1095, changed the face of Europe and the Middle East. The Crusades were a Holy War against the Infidel—the Arab Moslems who held Jerusalem. These Holy Wars changed the world politically, economically, so- cially, intellectually, and demographically. One can no more ignore the link between the Crusades and the Catholic Church than one can ignore the effect of rain on grass.

Often the people on the other end of Western religion's terrible swift sword were people of color whose lands Europeans stole in the name of Mission, Progress, Colonies, the White Man's Burden, and Manifest Destiny. Much of this history tears at us today; much we would like to forget.

The experience of violence and war made us who we are.

The ancient Hebrews were warriors. The Bible's first five books are full of images of battle, from the full-scale trumpets at Jericho's walls to the single slingshot David used to fight Goliath. The Jewish holiday Chanukah commemorates a battle, the Macabee uprising against the Syrians. The miracle, that oil intended for one night lasted during eight nights of worshipful resistance, is a miracle of strength. Strength, bravery, confidence, these are virtues modern Israelis have tried to reclaim. Battle has made them, too, who they are, for better and worse.

Although the 1982 Episcopal Hymnal has no more military pictures and the hymn "Onward Christian Soldiers" is gone from its pages, the meaning of American faith is still shaped by the memory of war. Church and war are intertwined in our history. The Civil War tore at America. Confederate memorials can be found in Southern churches. And while we can give up the warrior's imagery and the warrior's words, we cannot give up the fact of war's influence. The First World War taught Americans what God looked like in the trenches. The Second World War told grateful Americans to build houses of worship; most churches in the United States date from after the Second World War.

We are so tied to war and warriors that we are not even sure how to live in a world without enemies. We are not sure where to find our heroes or our strength. We abhor violence, but we fear weakness. We are not sure how to live with others, but we are even less sure how to accept ourselves.

One lesson we could profit from is forgiveness. The Catholic Church, a forgiving church, understands human frailty and accepts all things as human. It is not necessary to forget the past only to forgive it. Then you can move beyond it to an ideal of peace. In this view, you don't lose sight of your ideals; you can still achieve them.

Another way of facing the past and the past's violence is

through understanding. The Episcopal Church is a church of reason. So the question is not how badly did I err, but were my intentions honest? Was it a good fight, a fight dictated by necessity, by justice, by reason? Did I believe in what I was doing? To fight and lose is no dishonor. To change your fight as reason teaches you anew is no dishonor. But to believe in nothing because it is safest that way, that is cowardice. You can say out loud, "I was wrong, but I was brave," and so choose peace at the same time that you honor past wars.

Also there is sympathy. The Jewish celebration of Passover, marking the Exodus from Egypt, recounts the plagues visited upon the ancient Egyptians in retribution for their treatment of the Jews. As each plague is named, a drop of wine falls to a dish, to represent the suffering of the victims of those plagues. At the same time that Jews rejoice for their freedom, they express sadness for the enemies they had to hurt. Happiness and sadness, pride and anguish—these go together. It is possible to be proud of the battle, but pained for the defeated. True, sometimes it is a strain to feel this sympathy for one's enemies. The Broadway show based on Sholom Aleichem's stories of Tevye the Milkman, *Fiddler on the Roof*, gave voice to the difficulty of feeling sympathy under extreme conditions. When one character asks the rabbi for a blessing for the czar, the best the rabbi can say is "May the Lord bless and keep the Czar . . . far away from us."

The past, with its wars and violence and anguish—and the present with its wars and violence and anguish—cannot disappear and need not disappear. There is no virtue in forgetfulness. There is virtue in the truth. Religions preach war and religions preach peace, but they mostly preach peace. That is and has been our ideal, even if we haven't always lived up to it.

The prophet Micah, after bidding everyone change their swords for plows, added that then each person should sit under his vine and under his fig tree and none shall make him afraid. Imagine that fig tree and that peaceful scene. So many of our shared hopes for America are held in that scene: the beautiful natural environment, the lack of fear, the feeling of plenitude, a place where none is wanting. Yet this picture is very different from Isaiah's—and the painter Hicks's—peaceable kingdom. The peaceable kingdom is crowded with animals and human beings in groups, all mingling and interacting, leading and following, lying together, looking at one another. Saint Paul saw peace as harmony when he described the world as neither Gentile nor Jew, male nor female, a world without divisions, but a world of plenitude. That scene expresses our shared hopes for America, too. We hope that people will come together, interact, learn from one another. So which is the image of peace? Is peace people together, or is peace one man alone under his fig tree?

And if one man sits alone under a fig tree, and each man and woman has his or her own tree, who would there be to make them afraid? Micah tells us that violence and fear go together, and where there is no violence, there will be no fear. But what is the implied threat under those fig trees that causes Micah to add "and none shall make them afraid"? Although there is always the threat of marauding armies, or some distant, unforeseen war, there is another message here. It is a message about the individual, alone, facing himself. Micah says, in a way, that when each man is safe, alone, and there is no more war and no more want, *and* when each man looks at his own capacity for destruction and stops *his own destruction of himself,* then, really, that is peace.

The reminder is the fig tree. Adam and Eve used fig leaves to hide their nakedness in the Garden of Eden. It is as if people are always saying to fig trees, "Save me from myself. Save me from my own wrongdoing, from my own capacity for evil." Now this is truly an American dilemma. We are a people who like independence. We seek peace in solitude, behind suburban lawns, city walls, and forest pines. Can violence or the capacity for violence exist where a man is absolutely alone? That is a strange idea to us Americans, who, along with the poet Robert Frost, believe "Good fences make good neighbors." Put up a fence. Give him a fig tree. Isn't that peace enough? No. We find that that is not peace enough. There can be violence, an inner destruction even for the man alone. Religion teaches peace because its province is the soul. Religion speaks to human violence, yes, but also to the human capacity for violence.

Each of us can destroy him- or herself in hundreds of ways. In fact, our own capacity for violence is great. We can sabotage our own ability to act by using drink or drugs. Or, without drink or drugs, we can deny our humanity by hating everyone and everything. Or we can destroy ourselves by hating ourselves and letting self-doubt cripple and deform us like a wasting disease. We can assert ourselves through violent acts, claiming power because we have the power to destroy.

Imagine the man under his fig tree. He has no enemies. There are no invading armies. He starts thinking, "I'm very powerful. I can do whatever I want." In fact, peace is starting to feel a little boring. He wants to show his power. He used to hurt people. That shows power, he thinks. But the people are gone. He looks around. "I'm so powerful, I can do anything I want. I could cut down this fig tree." He cuts down his own fig tree. Now he has no shield from the harsh sun, no fruit to eat, no beautiful tree to enjoy. Such a man is not really at peace, according to Micah's image. He is a threat to himself, so in fact, there still is something to make him afraid. Himself.

It is in this way that Saint Paul explains to the Corinthians that demonstrations of power are not power at all. He says, When I am weak, then am I strong. He says that true power belongs to God, not to us earthen vessels, the humans that carry His message. We are troubled and cast down, but the power to act may not be the remedy. Saint Paul speaks of the outward man and the inward man. The outward man acts. The outward man fights back. The outward man must assert his will, his power. The outward man conquers. The outward man builds. The outward man fights, dies, perishes in bloody battles.

So far America has been the outward man. We have had a bloody history, amassed land, built weapons, vanquished foes, but also killed friends, destroyed our environment, destroyed our own people, and destroyed ourselves. Now it is time to reflect. There are no more frontiers. Looking inward is our frontier now. On the one hand, we want to end violence. On the other hand, we want to understand our own capacity for violence. Religion does not only ask, "How can we stop violence?" Religion asks, "Why are we violent?" We keep asking because even when the violence goes away, the question doesn't.

America needs to look inward and start a period of reflection and understanding. The period of conquest is over. Just as individual self-awareness and understanding comes late, after the action and conquests of youth, our nation's self-awareness is only now beginning, after conquest, triumphs, and power. Self-awareness will end violence, not only the violence of war, but also our violence toward ourselves, our meaningless shows of power. The problem is, do we as a nation know how to do this? What is self-awareness in a nation? Do we as individuals even know how to think about ourselves?

Our shared tradition suggests three ways religion can help in this process of looking inward. First we can turn to the narratives and parables, some of the most dramatic, the most tragic, the most deeply moving that we have available to us. Religion has played an important storyteller's role, and stories speak clearly to people. Good advice and admonitions assume a rational, critical audience, but our view of ourselves is not always rational and critical. Sometimes it is. Often it isn't. Sometimes the rational, critical interpretation of our past is too literal and simplistic. Someone might say, "My great-grandfather owned no slaves. Why should I take second place to a descendant of African slaves when I did him no harm?" It sounds rational, it sounds critical, but it has nothing to do with the complete story of the United States, its rise to wealth, and its continued legacy of racism. Religion can help Americans understand themselves and their country by supplying the narrative, telling the stories that then let Americans feel connected to one another and to a cultural past. At the same time, these narratives and metaphors let listeners draw their own lessons.

There are stories in movies, stories on television; there are novels. And each of us has his or her own story, the way we explain what has happened to us and who we are. Some of these stories are shared. Some are so private only you alone might know them. But America requires a different kind of story. America requires a story with God in the telling. America requires its next understanding. We were once a city on a hill, but we are not now. We were once the vehicle of a manifest destiny, but we are not now. Who are we now? The answer will be in America's relation to God, and it will be the story of an inward-looking America.

When we know that story, we will tell and retell it, and it will have more power because religion is participatory, shared. A rabbi whose grandfather had been a disciple of the Baal-Shem Tov was asked to tell a story. "A story," he said, "must be told in such a way that it constitutes help in itself."

And so he said: "My grandfather was lame. Once they asked him to tell a story about his teacher. And he related how the holy Baal-Shem Tov used to hop and dance while he prayed. My grandfather rose as he spoke, and he was so swept away by his story that he himself began to hop and dance and show how the master had done it. From that hour he was cured of his lameness. That's the way to tell a story."

We will tell a story of America so powerful that when we tell it we will be transformed in the telling. It will move us to act as the story instructs, yet it will move us emotionally, not just rationally. What will this new story be? We know some of the elements already: a nation of many peoples, where freedom triumphed over slavery and kindness over hatred. But the story isn't written yet, and it has yet to move us in the telling.

The second way religion can help Americans look inward is by helping America change the way it faces outward. Just as we need a new story, because the United States is no longer the center of the world, we need a new organization to recognize our interconnectedness with the rest of the world. Now is the time for American religions to join in concert with the religions in other countries to start this process of looking inward, of finding solutions rather than empty shows of power. Here, too, self-awareness will work in the service of peace. As we understand others, we will understand ourselves. As we understand ourselves, we will become sensitive to others.

Religion can do this if we only have the organization. In Bosnia-Herzegovina, early in the conflict, the American envoy Cyrus Vance gathered the heads of the Muslim, Roman Catholic, and Greek Orthodox faiths together, hoping that the religious leadership of the region would not give in to tribal or ethnic animosities, but would find some common ground for peace. He thought that these groups could use their moral influence to make more choices available to people. And he was successful in getting the leaders together. Once they were there, though, the religious leaders screamed at each other for two hours. And Vance said, "The meeting is over. But I need to tell you how disappointed I am. Because there are so many lives at stake, and you are all the heads of religions here. And all you could do was yell at each other. Why?" They said, "What do you mean? We always yell at each other."

The time for such moral bankruptcy is past. Now America's religious groups can join with the world's religions to accept moral accountability. America's religious organizations can help Americans look inward by no longer passively echoing jingoism and airing it in the pulpit. What if the world's religions united in taking moral accountability? What if they said, "We are responsible for each life on this planet, and we urge you to choose peace, not war"? Americans could then understand themselves in a moral world and in a united, interconnected world.

Third, American religion can help America change its course by providing an education in values. The story of America can help us explain ourselves to ourselves; the global outlook will increase our sensitivity. But we will not remember who we are if we do not remember what it is we stand for. Our people must know right from wrong. Our children must know that there is a right way and a wrong way to go about things. This is such an important idea that it bears examination.

Under the flag of values education educators have closed their eyes and ears and minds to new ideas. Under the guise of values education teachers have deemed themselves censors and have turned students into intellectual prisoners. Under the cover of values education, parents have chosen ignorance over awareness and have ignored rather than guided their children.

No.

That is not what we mean.

The only way to understand your own beliefs, the only way to let the inward human being be renewed day by day, is through the free exchange of ideas. What we mean by values education is not the rote learning of one point of view, but the ongoing discussion about ideas we cherish. Values education is not punitive; it does not mean punishing a child for trying out a new idea. Rather it is the very time-consuming process of pointing the way again and again and again.

Is it true that children today have lost a sense of right and wrong? Is it true that violence among children is more prevalent than ever? Perhaps what children have lost is parents and grandparents. Have they lost their values? Or did they not have values to begin with? They do not need prisons, literal or intellectual; they need schools. How much more efficient, more reasonable, more economic—and more human, more loving, and more decent—it would be to teach right and wrong before prison even becomes a question. Teaching values takes time. It takes time to repeat the lessons, it takes time to have the discussions, it takes time to absorb new ideas, and it takes time to respond to criticism. It takes time for parents to be with their children; it takes good childcare arrangements, fair family-leave programs at work, and flexible work hours. It takes time for teachers to show interest and patience—it takes a living wage for teachers, extracurricular programs in schools, and free intellectual exchange. Only then can we instill in all Americans the ideas that have sustained us: community, caring, faith, courage, love of the earth, equality, freedom. These are our values, not the hatred, not the empty glory, not the self-centeredness of an isolationist America. Education is our mainstay and our hope for the future. This issue is so important that we will discuss it alone in the next chapter.

VII

Counting Seasons

*There is childishness where
there should be wisdom.*

First consider an immigrant's tale.

Lily Kaufman had only one child, but she had had many miscarriages. She was an immigrant in that generation of immigrants who arrived early in this century and lived to near its end. Loss and hardship were familiar to her, but so was passion. She and her future husband exchanged ardent letters until, finally, she left New York City and joined him to settle in New Haven. She was a serious, shrewd woman, a worrier. Sparkle and coquetry were luxuries she had never had. Her mother was sick, her sisters studied and taught, her father was no more than a middling businessman. He had so hated the United States that he took the whole family back to Grodno. But one final bad experience set Lily's mind. Feeling very American, she asked a Russian policeman for directions and he spit at her in response. She left Russia, this time alone, determined to live in the United States. Her parents and sisters followed, dependent upon her strong will and her competence.

She married and moved to New Haven. Her sisters never married and had no children. Lily had just the one daughter. She wanted for her daughter the best, the most important things in life. But what did that mean? Yiddish. Definitely Yiddish. Her daughter must attend special after-school Yiddish classes. How else could she understand her culture and remain part of her parents' world? Yiddish was the language of the love letters, of all the letters, neatly stored, packed away and kept. But no. Her daughter cried. She hated the classes, it was too hard, no one else had to go, she refused. She was willful, her daughter.

Her daughter wanted to go away to college. She wanted to be a teacher. She wanted an education. Lily argued. Sure, an education. So you can forget us. She knew all about education. She secretly feared that her daughter would end up like her sisters, educated and alone. There was an understanding more im-

portant than school; there was the knowledge of human relationships—love, marriage, children. Had she worked so hard to have a family only to leave her daughter to a life of loneliness? And herself to an old age of loneliness?

It all ended happily, even after the terrible fights. Lily's daughter did go away to school and did become a teacher. She came back, though, and married someone so trustworthy and competent that even Lily could let down her guard. There were two beautiful grandchildren. Lily even lived to see her grandson marry a serious girl, a worrier. He was very smart, her grandson. In this puzzle of American life, though, it was hard to say exactly what that meant. Would he remain a Jew? Would he earn a living? Would he make the right decisions? Culture, education, wisdom—it is all a puzzle of American life.

VALUES

We have called this work a book of values. Values are ideas that are important to us. Everyone has values, although we might not agree with other people's values, or we might believe those values to be the wrong values. That is like the dying man who thought he saw his life passing before his eyes, only it was the wrong life. It is now fashionable to discuss values; the question is, are they the wrong values? It is not true that some people have values and others do not. Someone might value excitement. Often it seems that our media value novelty. "Man bites dog" is a better story than "Dog bites man." Excitement and novelty don't sound like the stuff of sermons and church picnics. Nevertheless, they can fall under the heading of values, and it's good to keep that idea in mind.

Should we instead use the heading "traditional values"? We have been discussing tradition, especially religious tradition. Still, it's important to remember that some very important ideas, very wonderful ideas, are modern rather than Biblical, and we use the word *traditional* as an honorary title, not a historical one. Foremost among these new-old values is friendship. Friendship is a strong

American value. Americans have friends, make friends, make new friends, teach their children to be friends, send greeting cards to friends, broadcast commercials featuring friends, make movies about friends, and understand history through stories about friendship. Friends are so important in this country that a political figure who can name no friends is suspect, lacking an essential element in his or her life.

One reason that friendship is so essential to American life is that it constitutes practice in interacting with others different from oneself. Friendship is actually practice in citizenship. Unlike the sibling, cousin, *paysan,* or *landsmann* of past centuries, the friend can come from another town or country or have had different experiences. If it's a quick friend in a time of need, it may be an American "buddy," in the trenches or in bad times (Buddy, can you spare a dime?) or a partner in the buddy system at school.

Is all this friendship traditional? Some people point to Jonathan and David as Biblical friends. Ruth and Naomi, although related through marriage, seem to have had some link of friendship. The philosopher Saint Thomas Aquinas wrote about friendship and its relationship to charity. He quoted the Gospel of Saint John where it says, "Henceforth I call you not servants . . . but I have called you friends." Saint Thomas Aquinas recognized that benevolence or good will or even seeking some good for ourselves, such as pleasant company, is not the same as seeking true friendship. Friendship is mutual—mutual liking or mutual love. Sometimes we experience the deep friendship Aquinas described, but often it's just plain old American buddies. And that's valued, too.

Mostly friendship as we think of it is a modern idea. The scholar George Mosse identifies it as a product of Enlightenment thought, a direct result of ideas of equality. Unlike the relationships developed in medieval Catholic religious orders or communities, friendships could be individual, secular, and unrelated to a larger institution or purpose. Still many friendships today, such as "old school ties" do have their origin in an institution.

As an expression of traditional American values, what better example is there than an Ivy League alma mater? Such songs are full of such friendship talk.

If friendship, enshrined in song and tradition and lived in almost every American's life, is such an important value, why don't we hear about it in political "values" discussions? Because it isn't threatened? Because it isn't news? Or because it isn't politically useful? The historian John Boswell once wrote that most of us never once in our lives encounter quicksand. It is so useful for disposing of inconvenient characters, however, that someone who read a fair amount and watched films might believe quicksand to be the greatest hazard facing Americans. In other words, if it's useful, it's news.

The phrase "family values" now seems very useful. Most of us have no idea what the phrase means. Families are no longer determined only by blood relationship; they are also built by links of trust and honesty; "societal values" is probably a more descriptive term. But the phrase "family values" is so useful for disposing of political enemies that someone who read a fair amount and watched television might believe that "family values" are of concern to Americans. The problem is, what does the term mean? A family itself is not a value, but an institution, an organized way of doing things. (We discussed institutions in Chapter 2.) Are family values the values that a family teaches, or values that make family life possible, or just a positive feeling toward the institution of the family? One of the values that American families teach is friendship, but that barely enters the debate. So let's carefully examine the idea of "family values" and the institution behind it, the family.

What is a family? Is it a ready-to-wear article, or a straitjacket, as some would have it? San Francisco columnist Rob Morse once quipped that the phrase "dysfunctional family" is redundant. He was thinking of that one-size-fits-all family summed up in the experience of a shoe salesman, many years ago, flabbergasted by his customer's request. "I want to buy shoes for my husband," a woman said. The salesman wanted to know how he could help find the right size if the husband wasn't there to try them on? "Oh, give me a ten," the customer said. "He wears an eleven, but my son's a nine, and they have to share them." Sometimes people discuss "the family" as if it were as big as IBM and twice as impersonal. They make it sound as if the shape or proper arrangement of components is all that matters.

A man once went to buy a suit, and after trying several he settled on one and ordered alterations. He returned to the store, full of optimism, and tried on the finished suit. But it was horrible; it bagged and bunched and pulled. It pinched, buckled, drooped, and sagged. Just as his shock turned to anger, the salesman intervened, "Try lifting your shoulder a little there. Perfect." The salesman positioned him in front of the mirror. "Now, you know, if you just stuck your leg out, it's really very good." When the customer had assumed the right pose he agreed; the suit was perfect. He left the store hobbling as the salesman had instructed him, one foot out, one shoulder up, and passed two commuters. "That poor man," one of them whispered, "what terrible shape he's in." The other one answered, "Yeah, but what a great suit."

If all families fit like cheap suits, keeping their own shape only to distort the lives of their members, the institution wouldn't be worth all that much. The family has endured thanks to its flexibility and resilience and its ability to conform to fit its members. Since the family takes many shapes, family values mean many things. The Episcopalian who gives his son his own name, the Catholic who cares for her ailing aunt, and the Jew who attends a holiday dinner are all demonstrating family values. The family has endured for its inclusiveness, its ability to mean many things. The family is one of the few places where human beings experience a sense of wholeness: the family is a protective retreat that nurtures children, incorporates mature adult sexuality, and cares for the elderly and infirm. "Family values," if the phrase means anything, means this sense of wholeness, each part helped, each person respected, over the course of a whole lifetime. When we say that we value the family, we mean that we value this wholeness, the respect for each individual and each individual's connection to others.

The conditions of family life do not always match our ideals. Some children may wish it could be their mother rather than their great-aunt who gives them breakfast. Some couples may wish for children but never have them. We may be freed of medieval rules of primogeniture, which granted full inheritance and consequently family rights to only the first son, but life has thrown up new reasons and obstacles to make us fall short of our ideals. But the world in its plenitude is full of ideas and full of roles for each one of us to play. We value the spirit, but not everyone is a member of the clergy. We value beauty, but not everyone is beautiful. We value families, but not everyone has children. Conservatives who would use the phrase "family values" as a cudgel and the family as a straitjacket do justice to neither the phrase nor the reality. A family is and has always been part of the larger world of community, church, and government, and just as no individual stands alone, no family stands alone.

In fact, the Bible is peopled with tribes, strangers, individuals, and exemplars more often than with nuclear family units. The nuclear family is a relatively modern invention. Instead of searching our tradition for some reference to what we call a family, let's look at what a family does. The value most necessary to family life, almost the very definition of family life, is privacy. The family atmosphere, after all, is the opposite of the push and bustle of social life. No matter how big the family, or, for that matter, how important, there is always a family us and a public them. Within the family there is the private joke, the private disagreement, the private financial arrangements. In the Jewish shtetls of Eastern Europe, community life was constant and vocal. Yet if a household disagreement became too intense, there was still the rebuke, "Do all the neighbors need to know the family's business?" The Jewish wedding ceremony sometimes includes the ritual of the bride walking seven circles around the groom to draw a symbolic circle of exclusivity. The adult sexual relationship, at the family's center, is apart from the world of other relationships.

In fact, privacy is such a central family value that the social historian Philippe Aries believed that modern privacy and the modern family grew at the same time, dependent one upon the other. There was a time, he wrote, when sexual relationships were public business. French kings before the revolution married to ensure heirs but openly supported pleasure houses. Kings' mistresses were more powerful public figures than their wives were. Also at that time kings would receive callers while in bed. What was good for society's best worked for its worst; the public tavern knew everyone's business, and a bed was such a luxury that an inn might put four or five paying guests in one. There was no such thing as a private room, let alone a private bath. In fact, baths were taken in public, as at the baths at Bath, England.

Eventually the push of the social world became intolerable, especially for the new middle classes who sought a different kind of life. The household became synonymous with the family, as the king's retinue was left at court. The family, alone together, was able to enjoy a life not possible elsewhere.

Father Joseph Keegan, S.J., a professor of psychology at Fordham University, in his essay "Privacy and Spiritual Growth," which appeared in a collection called *Privacy: A Vanishing Value?* wrote about the importance of family privacy. First of all, without question, Catholic confession is protected and inviolable, not only because it is a matter of Catholic law, Father Keegan explains, but because it is necessary that the individual have a "core," a "core of the life of the spirit." Everyone, he explains, has unrealized goals, gaps in his beliefs, skills he'd like to use but hasn't, all the ingredients necessary for continuing to grow. These are part of an inner core of privacy.

But more. The family protects this delicate core. He says that within the family the child's need for privacy can be recognized, because within the family the child can meet patience and acceptance. The outside, public world laughs at mistakes and reprimands mishaps. The family, though, loves its own and gives its members the feeling of self-worth necessary to feel spirituality—that is, to feel loved by God.

At least, that is the hope and the reason privacy is a necessary moral value. In the name of privacy, husbands have abused wives and parents have abused children. The fresh air of outside contacts keeps families sane and safe; too much privacy is as harmful as too little. All we know is that some privacy is central to our lives.

Just what constitutes privacy is another matter. As the sociologist Barrington Moore Jr. succinctly put it, ideas of privacy tend to be influenced by the amount of space available in combination with the available plumbing. The less space you have, the more plumbing you need. Apartment-dwellers in Manhattan make do with a tiny fraction of the space needed by Mbuti pygmies, and consequently they require hundreds of times the plumbing. In fact, Moore says, on matters of sex, personal hygiene, and bodily functions, people make do with all kinds of arrangements and make do pretty well. What they cannot abide is large-scale public intrusion into private matters. That is why Western law and society have developed safe-guards to protect the many from intruding on the privacy of the few.

Religious minorities have long relied on the family to do the job of protecting people from external pressure. When a family pratices a minority religion, they rely on themselves to keep the traditions alive. A story is told of a dying man who wants his last blessing. He asks for the clergyman of the town's biggest church, the church of the majority religion. The old man's son is furious. "After all these years you taught us to stand up for our own faith—and now this. Why do you want a different clergyman?" the son cries.

"I want to convert," the man answers.

"Convert? How can you say that? After all these years . . ."

"Look, I'm dying," the old man reasons. "I figure better one of them dead than one of us."

Sometimes, though, the threat of public pressure has been more immediate and intense. Those countries most hostile to the family have been precisely those most hostile to privacy—totalitarian regimes where children are encouraged to spy on their parents. Not coincidentally, governments hostile to the family and hostile to privacy are also hostile to religious expression. Communist China or the former Soviet Union, for example, outlawed religion and privacy with it, as well as attacked the family.

Barrington Moore Jr., an expert on totalitarianism and the Soviet Union and a teacher at Harvard, strongly argues that the Western legal tradition has guaranteed privacy, and other values, as well. Moore is the descendant of a prominent Episcopalian family. His nineteenth-century forebear, Clement Moore, wrote the famous "Visit from St. Nicholas" poem, combining old Dutch New York legends and American traditions. As a student at Yale, Barrington

Moore fell ill and had to take time off from classes. A professor suggested he spend his time studying Russian: "It will be an important country someday." During the Second World War, Moore worked in the Office of Special Services, that is, intelligence. He claimed that the best training for intelligence work was the study of Classics. Why? Because intelligence work was the study of fragments, more like the study of an ancient text that comes to you in pieces than the study of a set of historical facts.

What was the link that made Moore, a political iconoclast, so proud of his family; this student of Classics, so concerned with modern politics; this fierce defender of merit, duty bound to teach a descendant of John Adams, whom Moore took into his class? Why did Moore choose to study privacy? He says himself in his introduction to *Privacy* that it was to see if everyone valued it as much as his culture did. We, this Western, Judeo-Christian culture, we value privacy.

So take a moment to consider this family value, privacy. When conservatives cry "family values," do they really mean that they just want more breathing space, for doubt and ambivalence, room to develop that private inner core? Or is it privacy as a way of escaping the social demands of helping the poor and the foreign? Or are they suggesting not a family value at all, but a way of telling others how to live their lives and a way to reduce the privacy of others? When the Right says "values" why don't they name privacy? Clinton Rossiter said, "The free man is the private man, the man who still keeps some of his thoughts and judgments entirely to himself." We can say, the free family is the private family, where external public pressure does not dictate private behavior.

෨

RESPECT FOR THE AGED IS ONE OF THE VALUES WE associate with family life. Honoring one's father and mother is one of the Ten Commandments, one of our primary rules of conduct. This means, first of all, that we are responsible for providing for their physical well-being. We are so steeped in this tradition, this way of looking at the world, that it is easy to forget that other peoples at other times have seen the aged differently. In some cultures, when the aged were no longer able to contribute to the work of the group, they were sent away or sent off to die. That is not Judeo-Christian teaching. In fact, the rabbis of the Sanhedrin, the ancient rabbinic court, considered "honoring" one's mother and father to mean not only supplying food, drink, clothes, and footwear, but also assisting their movements so that they might go where they would. Why are we so committed to providing this assistance? Today in the United States people talk of a generational war; many among the young don't want to pay the taxes to support the retirement and medical costs of the old. Yet a caring society respects its aged.

Age is a state of weakness, and we care for the weak among us. While it is possible to list the infirmities that beset the old, such wisdom hardly moves us. Many old people today don't seem "old," and for those do, medical technology promises miracles. Are they really weak after all? Or is that an outdated view?

Two golfers, depressed about the onset of weaknesses that would hurt their game, vowed to play together. One could not walk well and was overly dependent on his cart. The other had trouble seeing. His swing was perfect, but he couldn't see where the ball was going. The first said, "Don't worry. My vision is perfect, and I'll find the ball for you." The game went well enough, their spirits buoyed by the partnership. In fact, their game improved. Finally, the man who had trouble seeing hit the shot of a lifetime. The ball sailed into the air, and his parner cried, "Don't worry. I see exactly where it went." They jumped into the golf cart to follow the ball. They rode and rode. The impatient golfer with poor eyesight said, "Well, where's the ball?" His partner with the eagle eye said, "I forgot."

In other words, one of the real weaknesses of advancing age is the difficulty in recognizing and accepting weaknesses. According to an old Jewish legend, there was no old age until Abraham. Fathers and sons were mistaken one for the other. Abraham, desperate to be honored for his age and experience, pleaded with God, "You must create age; you must create some visible distinction between father and son." So when Abraham awoke the next morning he had white hair and a white beard. "God, is this the sign you have given me as a mark of old age? It is unattractive. It is hideous. I don't like it." Abraham, willing to accept a sign of age, was unprepared for *this particular* sign. Like most of us. The sign we get is not always the one we hoped for. Is age weakness? Yes. It is weakness in the face of a difficult task: acceptance.

We respect the aged not only for their weakness, but for their strength, because we value each individual life. In our society there is no individual who is expendable, no one we would send out to sea because she or he can no longer contribute. Rather, as the very old approach death, frequently they teach others the meaning of life. We respect the aged for their wisdom and experience. The chronicler of early England, the monk Bede, describing a dye he had seen said, "The older the cloth, the more beautiful the color."

You may think, But this is too much. My aged relatives don't match your characters. They don't have the patriarch's flowing white beard. They don't talk in Biblical prose of wisdom and life. They are not beautiful at all. When they don't speak, they drool, and when they do speak, they don't listen, running willy-nilly, yelling, "Quick, someone ask me a question. I have such a great answer." What's more, they did not pass an admirable youth.

Catholic tradition emphasizes the enormity of the gift parents give their children, the gift of life. There is no greater gift, and a lifetime of gratitude is not enough to repay this special, singular gift. Honor, respect, love, obedience, and gratitude in uncountable quantities are due to those who have extended God's work of creation. As the apostles Mark and Luke observed, Jesus promised peace and harmony to those who would honor their parents.

There is an intuitive truth here. Most people seem to feel it just from observing the world. Some people seem better at getting along with other people. How do they do it? They have long, close friendships or maybe many good, reliable acquaintances. They don't fight much; they don't get too angry. They don't infuriate their parents. They try to keep in touch with relatives. Sure enough, when they need a favor, someone's there. If they're down on their luck, someone will help them out. They might be remembered in someone's will. You're tempted to look at these people's social skills and say, "If only they could bottle that!" Not everyone has such skills. And sure enough, the son or daughter who rejects his or her parents has a tougher road. The homeless man without the ability to make attachments becomes a drifter. The poor woman who can't get a neighbor to help her with the kids becomes overwhelmed.

We don't really know why some people seem to have more of this ability to connect than do others. All we know is that there is a wisdom thousands of years old that says, If you try to keep these family ties, life will go better for you. Or at least life could go better for you. You could be stronger.

The family respects the aged because, good or bad, they are their history, their link to time. And in our shared religious tradition time, the counting of seasons, matters. We move through time toward progress, toward a better world, toward the Kingdom of God, or the Second Coming, or the Messiah. We move toward the future, and we remember the past. Families matter. Ancestors matter. Exodus, describing the flight of the ancient Hebrews from Egypt, says, "Moses took with him the bones of Joseph, who had exacted an oath from the children of Israel, saying, 'God will be sure to take notice of you: then you shall carry up my bones from here with you.'"

Centuries later rabbis found scant drama and ceremony in this Biblical account. They wrote a Midrash—their speculation of what may have occurred as Moses and the Israelites feverishly planned their departure from Egypt. The rabbis imagined Moses attempting to fulfill the promise made to Joseph by frantically searching for Joseph's remains, even at the very moment that the Israelites were busy stuffing their possessions into sacks and containers. After a hurried search, Moses learned that the Egyptians had hidden the remains in the Nile—not only to allow the body of this revered leader to consecrate its waters, but, more important, to prevent the Israelites from leaving Egypt because of the promise made to Joseph.

Learning of Joseph's burial in the Nile, Moses raced to its shores and called, "Joseph, Joseph, the time has come in which God swore to redeem Israel, as has the time of the fulfillment of the oath you had Israel swear to you. Israel is waiting for you." With those words Joseph's coffin bobbed up to the surface. Moses retrieved it and took it with him on all his desert wanderings until it could be delivered to the Promised Land.

So all the while the Israelites wandered through the desert they carried two boxes: one containing the tablets of the Law and the other the bones of Joseph. Were the boxes heavy? Often when people talk of "excess baggage" they mean the burdens of past expe-

riences, which they carry around with them. Individuals bear the
weight of their calamities, mishaps, ordeals, and hardships, no matter where they go or with whom they travel. Those who carry excess
baggage aren't able to get past unhappy events. Moses, though,
carried the bones of Joseph to draw closer to his ancestor.

Most of us don't have to search for the bones of our ancestors
as Moses did; they are in us, fused to our own bones. For some of us
the weight of ancestors' bones creates an inner tension because the
bones are an unwanted burden. But for others, those bones provide
comfort and strength.

In ancient Israel people were identified by name as the son or
daughter of certain parents. To this day, a Jewish child's Hebrew
name still includes *ben* or *bat*, the son or daughter of so-and-so,
linking the child to a chain of family members. Carrying those
names is like carrying the bones of Joseph; it provides a kind of
strength.

We have gone from honoring one's parents to respect for the
aged to respect for the dead. These traditions follow one upon the
other in a natural progression, for the family is the place for such a
natural progression. The family is the place for remembering, for
keeping history. New members take the names of older members.
They carry the bones, literally, figuratively, and symbolically. All of
this is very good and very important as long as the family keeps its
wholeness, its balance. "Family values," after all, means wholeness. If
love of the dead overpowers love of the living, there is no future. If
ancestor worship takes the place of looking forward to a better time
to come, then there is no hope. Change, too, is one of the elements
of our tradition.

The Episcopalian openness to the avant-garde has deeply
influenced our nation, moving it forward politically, intellectually,
and artistically. The Episcopal love of ancestry has been balanced

by love of change to produce not only political visionaries like Theodore and Franklin Roosevelt, but also artists such as Mary Cassatt. Mary Cassatt was not only a famous painter and not only the first and possibly most famous American woman recognized as a painter, but also she was the moving influence behind American art collection. She convinced collectors to invest in impressionist works by Degas and others and was the force behind the world-renowned Havemeyer family collection.

Mary Cassatt worked diligently, incessantly, from the time she was seventeen and began art school in Philadelphia in 1861, through her long career in Paris. She painted eight hours a day. Her strength was draftsmanship, not invention. Or at least that was the opinion of her friend and mentor, Edgar Degas. Her brother, Alexander Cassatt, was a trained engineer and a "railroad man"; he became president of the Pennsylvania Railroad.

Cassatt's family didn't have all that much money. It was just that her father was willing to take risks, to face the future. He had little, bought and sold what he had, but invested most heavily in what mattered most, his children. By educating his children in taste, beauty, hard work, and other lessons—achievement, independence, integrity, dignity—he created independent thinkers who contributed to the nation by embracing the future and facing the unknown. This theme of work and the idea that beauty inspires work we recognize as part of our national life, as *us*. It's almost as if the very definition of good taste is beauty in the service of work. And Mary Cassatt represented taste. The union of beauty and work is an American ideal.

The idea of transformation and the importance of the new is in Revelation: "See, I am making all things new," and in the broader understanding of Anglicanism. Urban T. Holmes III wrote, "Repentance is not just feeling sorry for our sins, but seeing the world in a new way. Jesus came to subvert our old outlook and give us new vision."

Memory and change, respect for the past, and love of the future, can be sides of the same coin. Memory, which sets humans apart from animals, can be useful or destructive. The repetition of certain behaviors, due to memory, may not be limited in time to a few months or years; it may ensnare succeeding generations. Since the business of the family is both past and future, we turn to another value associated with the family: nurturing children.

Just as the aged represent the past, children are the future. Religion's attitude toward children represents its optimism toward the future. The instruction to "be fruitful and multiply" is actually another way of saying to recognize that the Earth is good; for human beings, as for all creatures, growth and goodness are joined. When food is plentiful, disease infrequent, and war absent, human beings are fruitful and do multiply. In times of optimism the birth rate soars; in times of trouble it drops. The Bible is consistent in its genealogies and generational accounts: a link to the future is crucial and represents humankind's only chance at improvement, perfection. Abraham himself does not enter the Promised Land, but his children do. Most parents have some moment of realization when they understand that their children will be their living hope. Their children will see things and hear things they will not. They will go places their parents cannot follow. Sometimes that realization is joyful, and sometimes it is sad. When the children enter that new world, their parents won't be there to help them.

All of this is in Biblical instruction. Children in the Bible are identified with their parents and their families. Biblical figures have many children. What is not in the Bible is a weekend touch football game, a minivan, and a trip to Toys "R" Us. In fact, for most of history, children were not the focus of adult life; they were little people expected to take up adult occupations at an early age, as early as three or four in the case of some farmwork. A shepherd boy might be eight or nine years old. A girl might have responsibilities for younger children at seven or eight. Although the importance of children is universally acknowledged, the meaning of childhood has varied over time.

Philippe Aries's classic, *Centuries of Childhood: A Social History of Family Life*, demonstrates that childhood as we think of it, as a tender age of intellectual discovery, physical change, and moral awakening, is a relatively new idea. Until about the seventeenth century, children in the Western tradition, once beyond babyhood (as late as four or five years old), moved through the adult world as little adults, with no special bedtime and no subjects appropriate to their attention. Even when ideas of childhood began to change in the 1600s and 1700s, children were still portrayed in early American painting as little adults, often stiff and serious and preferably silent. Children were not exempt from moral behavior or considerations of salvation. And as for physical change, adolescence was not discussed as a separate stage of development until this century.

So when conservative critics refer to "traditional" family values and cite their concern for children, we must ask, which tradition? When? Which children? Only the children whose parents can afford minivans? Or all children, everywhere, as Jesus meant when He said the children should come to Him? Only the children whose parents can afford nannies and swing sets? Or all children, as the prophet Isaiah said that all widows and orphans would be welcomed by the people of Israel? Do these "family" conservatives mean only white American children of the 1990s are worth discussing, or do they include those who even today are migrant farmworkers at eight or nine years old and family breadwinners at twelve?

Enduring family values, in Western tradition, do not include a specific program for child rearing. Much as we might like the idea of family or child to include our own sensibilities, the enduring meaning of concern for children has only three elements: physical well-being; a place of refuge, warmth, and acceptance; and preparation for life as a competent adult. Religion has helped the family accomplish these goals. Not every family focuses equally on all three. Not every family interprets these three goals the same way. Not all religions emphasize the same goals. Yet these are the ways we turn our children into our future. These are our family values.

Concern for children means ensuring that all children in our country are adequately fed, clothed, vaccinated, healthy, safe from physical harm, and strong enough to contribute to our national future. As our national social safety net disappears, there will be a destruction of family life the likes of which have not been seen in this century. When the government succeeds in erasing welfare payments and rescinding money for food, the first result will be poor people's inability to pay rent. As a result of this, families will double and triple up, increasing overcrowding to a point where privacy, and consequently healthy family life, cannot exist. Under such conditions people take to the streets and children are raised on the curb, between the trash cans.

But even the minimum of keeping kids off drugs and tobacco and persuading them not to drink and drive—if only this physical concern were accomplished in its totality, our children would face different, enriched lives. Can you imagine an America where every single child sparkled with health and energy and optimism? Where the American workforce would be strong and dependable? And the health costs for adults would go down?

Wait, you say, what business is this of mine? What happened to privacy? Can't the family feed its own mouths and wash its faces? No. That's why we don't call it family values; we call these societal values. If your children are vaccinated, mine will stay healthy. If my children stay off drugs, yours will be safer from violent crime. You don't have to be a parent to recognize in America's children a whole country's future.

Children need a refuge of warmth and acceptance. That is one ideal of family life. In the book of Jewish tradition, *Sayings of the Fathers*, Jewish men are instructed to treat their children kindly, to listen to them patiently. Historically the family has sometimes, but far from always, been such a refuge. Churches and synagogues, on the other hand, have often been such places. They have been places where very young people could experience awe and dignity, grandeur and beauty—sights and sounds that are not always made available to children. Celebrations like First Communion or a bar or bat mitzvah have given children attention and a feeling of importance. Through songs and stories children could express sorrow or regret, long before the free expression of feelings was widely accepted. And all of this went on through ages when family discipline was not always warm and the home was not always a place of acceptance.

Many families have recently become more sensitive and nurturing, more open to their children's feelings and ideas, and more interested in developing children's self-esteem. At the same time, more families are compound families, created after one or two previous divorces and marriages. That is a fact of American life. Rather than say "Value children," let's say "WE value children." In an unsteady world, churches and synagogues provide safe havens for kids who need a place to do their homework, for kids who want an ear, and for kids who just never get to see much beauty or to feel very important.

Should the whole world be made child-safe? Or, rather, should children be prepared for lives as competent adults? The first question is temporary, time bound, and variable. The second question, the enduring one, is the one that matters. Parents and societies have tried to prepare children for the future they would face, whether that meant taking them into the fields, teaching them by rote, or showing them examples of proper behavior. Keeping children from ideas you don't like does not work as well as teaching them ideas you do like. Values, accumulated, preserved, passed on —that is culture.

THERE IS AN AMBIVALENCE ABOUT WISDOM AND learning in our shared culture. Adam and Eve ate from the tree of the knowledge of good and evil. One consequence of disobeying God's command was the pain women feel in childbirth, a pain known nowhere else among living creatures. Learning is difficult, and wisdom can bring unspeakable sadness and longing. The preacher in Ecclesiastes, often believed to be the wise Solomon, says, "I applied my heart to know wisdom, and to know madness and folly: I perceived that this also was a striving after wind. For in much wisdom is much grief: and he that increaseth knowledge increaseth sorrow." And also, "of making many books there is no end; and much study is a weariness of the flesh." Saint Paul asks, "Hath not God made foolish the wisdom of this world? . . . God hath chosen the foolish things of the world to confound the wise; and God hath chosen the weak things of the world to confound the things which are mighty." In letters and legends and stories, our wisest observers question the value of wisdom.

At the same time, time and the passage of time, and the increase of knowledge, are everywhere in our Bible. The stories take shape in order, each order has a logic: figures appear, live, and die, to be replaced by others. The ministry of Jesus precedes his crucifixion; this observation sounds so obvious, so accustomed to time and order are we. Time is so important to us that we endlessly note its passage. Only the fool makes no note of time. Wisdom, then, however sad or painful, is preferable to foolishness. At least if we remember, we know who we are. "The wise man's eyes are in his head," Ecclesiastes also says, "and the fool walketh in darkness." For thousands of years our first necessity was to remember who we were, to remember the stories, and to preserve them over time.

THE PRESERVATION OF CULTURE

For a long time it was the task of religion to preserve culture, to keep alive knowledge and traditions that otherwise could be lost. People today use the phrase "culture wars" to describe the deep divisions within America over basic beliefs such as life's beginning or the expression of sexuality. Early culture wars were entirely different. They centered on the power of symbols, who had access to them, who was denied access. There was always a priestly or scholarly class. There was always a group of people more aware of life's mysteries or more interested in the subtleties of law or philosophy. They knew the words to say, the stories to tell, and the steps to take. They told the stories in any way they could, so that people would remember and the culture would not be lost. These religious figures turned their stories into haunting chants, moving parables, rhymes, rituals, and admonitions. They carved them in stone and illustrated them in stained glass beautiful and powerful enough to stir any imagination and fix any memory. There was one symbol, though, that early religious leaders could neither control nor contain: the written word. Whoever had it, had power.

What is so special about the written word? To reflect on it, take the example of this book. We are nearing the end of a journey. We have taken it together, readers and writers, and kept each other's

company—although we may be miles or even years apart. We have
gotten to know one another, thought about each other. Made one
another angry. Grown impatient. Grown to trust one another. A
hundred times the authors have sworn defeat, and a hundred times
the reader has vowed revenge. This is disastrous, one or the other
shouts. This is beautiful, one or the other murmurs. All about tiny
black marks on paper, symbols of the most abstract kind. These tiny
little lines and squiggles can move human beings to tears, can
change their thinking, change their lives. But if you want to, you are
free to return to the words again and again. You may stop at one
sentence, at two. You may save no more than one idea, but stare at
those words as long as you like. As you stare, you can add to the
page your own ideas, as if the words invite you to add more. In that
way even the oldest tale is new when it is committed to paper.

Many of the West's early culture wars were about the power
of the written word. The Hebrews were not sure it was God's will
that the Bible be translated into Greek. Hebrew was the language of
God's chosen people, they argued. Would translation destroy the
word of God? Seventy translators in seventy rooms were put to
work, and, sure enough, they created the same translation, using the
same words. This convinced the people that the meaning would not
be lost and that it was, indeed, God's will that the word of God be
read in other languages.

For centuries Catholic monks painstakingly copied written
texts in order to preserve knowledge and traditions. This copying,
which we now consider the very essence of monastic activity—
quiet, contemplative, spiritual—could be thrilling, dangerous, even
illegal. Who had the Word had power. In the sixth century of the
Common Era a priest named Columba went from Ireland to Britain
to preach the word of God to the northern Picts. The Picts gave
him in gratitude an island, Iona, on which to found a monastery.

The chronicler Bede, writing years later, was sure to mention that Columba was not a bishop, but only a priest and a monk. While at Iona Columba asked a higher church official if he might borrow his book of Psalms. Borrow, but not copy, the prestigious clergyman warned his inferior. When Columba returned the work, the church-man was angry. "You have had it too long. You copied it. You must turn over to me that copy." In history's first copyright decision, Columba was ordered to turn over his copy under the principle "To every cow belongs its calf."

For hundreds of years culture wars and wars over the Word were indistinguishable. Protestors like Martin Luther wanted the Bible printed in the vernacular, not just in Latin, so it could be accessible to broad masses of people. This was only possible at all because of Johannes Gutenberg's recent invention of the printing press. As literacy grew, a scholarly elite could no longer control or monopolize the word of God, or any word, for that matter.

The preservation of culture, while still a function of religion, does not have the same meaning today as it did when people could not read and the written alphabet was a magical, powerful set of symbols. Today the preservation of culture means keeping alive ideas and values, as we have tried to do in this book. Ideals of decency, charity, tolerance, kindness, peace, and faith are part of our culture, and we are proud of them. But there is no war to wage; there is no enemy. We want merely the freedom for each man or woman to be his or her best self. That involves education, not the preservation of any one culture.

The preservation of culture has now taken a backseat to education. We can educate within our own religious traditions. We can educate about certain ideals or values. The goal of education in a pluralist America, however, cannot be the mere preservation of one culture or any culture. We can no more give American students a limited diet of texts than we can demand that they produce illuminated manuscripts. Where once that was the cutting edge of scholarship, it is no more. The preservation of culture and education are two different things.

EDUCATION

We have taught and continue to teach children to be Catholics or Jews or Episcopalians. Catholic teaching orders were largely established as a response to the immigrant community in the United States, and these orders accomplished several things within the Catholic community. First, they expanded the role of women in the American Catholic Church far beyond what it had been in Europe. They provided low-cost education, including education in English-language and civics, which helped newcomers assimilate. These learning centers also preserved the Catholic religious tradition, as well as provided a focal point and a unifying experience for generations of Catholics. Stories of the school nuns fill the memories of many Catholics. The nuns were objects of infinite mystery and speculation. They were strict or indulgent, slovenly or fastidious, none too bright or sharp as a tack. Above all they instilled in many Catholics a respect and love for teaching as a treasured service to the community, as well as a deep love of learning. Teaching was a mission, and learning was a value. For many Americans, Catholic education, reaching from the smallest local school to the most advanced research university, was a testament to the relationship between religion and learning.

The idea of God and the love of God was for many years the very purpose of American education. Many of this country's oldest colleges and universities, including Harvard and Princeton, were established with the intention of educating ministers. The Bible's book of Proverbs says, "train your young ones in the way they should go; they will not swerve from it even in old age." Talmudic interpretation understood "young ones" to mean teenagers, either from sixteen to twenty-two years of age or eighteen to twenty-four years of age. Talmudic scholars felt that these were the years that shaped character. They were years of blossoming independent thought, when young people need direction more than ever. Interestingly enough, other observers noticed the same need for direction at this crucial age. Modern psychologists have identified the eighteen-year-old as a young idealist whose moral conscience is awakening. And Episcopalian educators who founded many college preparatory schools and colleges also recognized this as a pivotal age. America's Jesuit high schools and universities address this youthful age of idealism and intellectual awakening.

Still, American education, even most of private American education, is secular. We are only now realizing how uneasy and uncomfortable the truce between culture and education has become. The goal of education may not be to preserve culture, yet an education absent of any historical or philosophical or religious context seems particularly barren. We run the risk of forgetting why it is that we love learning, why we teach our children, the very meaning of study or curiosity. For we don't just teach; we prize teaching. We don't just vote on school budgets and carpool and sign yearbooks. Education is one of our deepest and oldest values.

The ancient Hebrew patriarchs, founders of monotheism, struggled to know their God, that divine presence who made the world just and showed them their path. God sometimes spoke to them and gave them instruction. God appeared in signs. But Jacob's understanding of God was different. Jacob's understanding of God came from a dream, a vision, a struggle within his own mind. Jacob had a thought about God. So it is with Jacob that a simple idea begins: it is thought that sets humankind apart. It is thought that allows humans to reach up to Heaven. It is thought that is the divine part of humankind, the part that God created in His image. Jacob's story says, Think, dream, and struggle and you will know God.

Study is not just an attribute of Jewish tradition; it is the very meaning of Jewish tradition. The tradition says that the world endures because of three activities: acts of loving kindness, worship of God, and the study of Torah. The study of Torah does not merely preserve the culture, although it surely does that. The study of Torah is the culture. Jews have been called the People of the Book. One reason for that is that Jews are the descendants of those ancient patriarchs who people the Old Testament. Another reason, though, is that Jews take the study of the book as their defining identity.

There is a legend of a cynical and derisive man who went from rabbi to rabbi, unwilling to study, but asking, "Will you teach me the Torah in a single rule?" Each rabbi was more insulted than the last at this sign of disrespect. Finally the man approached the famous Rabbi Hillel. "Will you teach me the Torah in a single rule?" Rabbi Hillel alone said yes. Any Torah is better than no Torah, any study better than no study, some understanding better than no understanding. Tradition admonishes: Don't wait until you have leisure to study; you may never have leisure. Don't say you do not have the ability. It is the study that matters, not the ability. Find a companion with whom to study. A lesson said four hundred times is better than one said three hundred times. Find a teacher. And think. As each human being learns and struggles to learn, he or she is like Jacob wrestling with the angel and drawing closer to God. The way to understand God, in most Jewish tradition, is to study. Rabbi Elijah ben Solomon, who lived over two hundred years ago, said, "If an angel were to show me all the mysteries of the Torah, it would give me little pleasure, because study is more important than knowledge. Only what we achieve through effort is dear to us."

By thinking and reading and studying human beings exercise the part of them that is divine. Thought is what sets us apart from animals and the animal part of ourselves. The Talmud advises young men to think about mathematics while in the bathroom. In other words, thought is a form of discipline.

The Jewish value on study served Jews over hundreds of years of forced relocations and evacuations. Education was a form of riches one could carry from place to place. It compensated for poverty when there were no riches at all. Thought was also a tool for survival. In one parable a general asks, "When will I defeat the Jews?" and his advisor responds, "Go to their schoolhouse. When you hear no more children's voices coming from the schoolhouse, then you will defeat the Jews."

The Passover Haggadah, the story of the flight from Egypt, has become the most popular and beloved of all Jewish books, so beloved that it can be found in dozens of different editions, styles, languages. The book is so close to Jewish hearts that more than four thousand Haggadoth have been catalogued and collected in libraries in Israel and throughout the world. Authors of Haggadoth have traditionally taken the opportunity to express the political climate of their times. So Israel's socialist kibbutz movement produced a Haggadah without God, and the 1927 *Moscow Communist Haggadah* declared, "May all the aristocrats, bourgeois, and their helpers . . . be consumed in the fire of the revolution." *The Haggadah of the Teachers*, from Odessa, Ukraine, in 1885, asked, "How does teaching differ from all other professions in the world?" (The text responds: "All the other professions enrich, and their practitioners eat and drink and are happy all the days of the year. But teachers groan and sorrow even on this night. In all other professions the workers do not dare to be brazen before their employers. But in teaching, the boys and girls disrupt, and yet all find the teacher to be guilty.")

If all this is true, and the Hebrew tradition of study was so important to survival, and it, in turn, influenced Western theology and on and on—if all of this is true, why was Lily Kaufman so worried about her daughter's studies? Why do we in America feel such ambivalence about education that we would warily pull away funds, try homeschooling, underpay our teachers, overfill our classrooms, censor textbooks? Like Lily Kaufman we fear for the end result. If this study doesn't preserve my own culture, then what is it? If this study doesn't make good people, then what is its purpose? Americans ask these questions right now. How does education fit into American life? Have we put a value on education?

American university education is arguably the best in the world. It is one of the best ventures America undertakes for its citizens. Also students the world over recognize an American university education as the best they can obtain. The credibility of American research universities stands unsurpassed. The research facilities, including laboratories and libraries, are both outstanding and accessible. More students can enter more libraries in American colleges and universities than anywhere in the world. The United States is by far the leader in accessible education, with its broad, diverse system of public and private institutions.

Do we love education in the United States? Yes, we do. We have an admirable history of the open exchange of ideas; not perfect, but admirable. Just as the country as a whole has benefited from the influx of energetic workers, American academies have benefited by accepting refugee scholars. Our universities take seriously the responsibility to create thinking citizens. The liberal education, that is, the broad course of study that teaches reasoning in many disciplines, is well and alive. Other countries may excel in technical apprenticeship programs, but the United States has clearly expressed its value on thought, study, questioning, discussion, and debate.

Education is the best export the United States has; an American education is a desirable commodity the world over, and students flock to the United States to spend their time and their dollars at American schools.

But this American monopoly on higher education is not guaranteed to last forever. Technology is eroding that monopoly right now. As computers make all libraries accessible with the shuffle of a mouse, actual physical access is less important. Critics of the American university system have become increasingly strident, focusing particularly on the complex role of the professor. In the struggle to both teach and do research, it is teaching that flags. There are disputes about curriculum. Most serious, however, is the prohibitive cost of a college education. Leaving aside for the moment problems of inequities of access, the prohibitive cost threatens to skew the meaning of education itself. Parents balk when they see C's and D's, and they groan, "But I paid so much." The cost of tuition does not buy grades, but as tuition rises, there is the temptation to read those grades differently.

Has this country expressed our value on education? No. For all of our exceptional higher education, we have not created communities that know how to teach young children to love learning. Where parents are under pressure economically, they view schools as a luxury. Where parents are under pressure in thousands of other ways, they come to expect more and more from the schools. Critics today argue that parents are less involved, that they do not attend parent-teacher conferences or check to make sure that their children are studying. It is not clear that farmers so eagerly gave up their children to studies a hundred years ago. In many parts of the United States, particularly in the Midwest, the school calendar is the agricultural calendar, designed around harvest and planting, so that children could still work the farms. But there is a difference between those farm parents and some parents today. There is also a difference between immigrant parents like Lily Kaufman and some parents today. While those earlier parents may not have liked the important role of schools, they did not demand of those schools that they do a parent's job. The clean handkerchief came from home. Today we are increasing our demands on elementary schools by threefold and cutting their resources by half.

America's lower schools are threatened by indifference. First, in the United States today teaching is declining as a respected vocation. As more prestigious careers open up to women, the many talented women who were once a captive workforce are moving away from teaching. This need not happen, except that we have not put our money where our values are—teachers are not highly compensated in the American scheme of things.

Second, there are glaring disparities between urban and suburban schools. Suburbanites support their schools with high property taxes. As the American people shift from city to suburb, they leave behind them discarded institutions, eroded tax bases, and dashed hopes.

And the government does not seem to care. There has been precious little public policy devoted to improving American elementary through high school education. Even President Bush's small "Beyond 2000" plan has fallen victim to budget conflicts within the Clinton administration.

The minimal standards for raising children—providing physical care, warmth and acceptance, and preparing them for adult life—are not met by the schools we ignore and underfund. Many American elementary schools struggle to keep weapons away from the building. Many do not have adequate chairs and desks, or other facilities. Bathrooms function as makeshift classrooms and closets as makeshift offices.

But the physical failures pale in comparison to the hostility surrounding education. Lawmakers have actually considered turning away from schools the children of illegal immigrants—a tragedy of unthinkable dimensions. For where would these children find acceptance, if not at school? Where would they *learn* acceptance, if not at school? And where would they prepare for life as Americans?

As for preparation, schools both rich and poor are failing at preparing their charges for life in a complex, diverse America. We need to teach the inner-city child and the rural child about the world outside in order for her to thrive; but we also need to teach the suburban child about the world inside. Parents and teachers have raised a whole generation not in schools, but in cocoons.

We need to commit care and resources to education in this country, just as we need to rethink health care. As with health care, the costs of education are growing astronomically. As with health care, selfish concerns are weakening public action. As with delivering health care, educating our children is both one of America's great strengths and one of its great weaknesses. As with health care, education is a vital public good, of benefit to the whole society.

And as with providing health care, educating our children has presented the American people with the most frustrating paradox. We have the buildings, the machinery, the personnel, the schedules, the licenses, bureaus, requirements, forms, procedures, and return envelopes. Why don't we feel better? Our hospitals are not making death any easier to bear, and our schools are not making us wiser. Here we are in a sophisticated world of high-tech hospitals and research universities. Life expectancy increases daily and access to university education is broad. At the same time, we are not surrounded by images of age and wisdom, but by images of eternal youth and stupidity. How is that possible? Is there no such thing as wisdom? We want to truly learn about life, to learn how to make good decisions, to learn how to appreciate the people around us, to learn what is important to us and to others.

VIII

Building Wisdom's House

There is suspicion where there should be solidarity.

There was once a king who sent out two messengers and with them two letters of introduction. With the first messenger the king sent a notice saying, "Believe whatever this man says, for he carries my ring and seal." With the other messenger the king sent the introduction, "Believe whatever this man says, whether or not he carries my ring and seal." The first messenger is like an educated person in our society—he has credentials and moves freely based upon those credentials. The second messenger's strength is not education, but wisdom. His understanding is not based on credentials or education alone, although he might very well have those as well.

WE HAVE, IN THIS BOOK, SET OURSELVES THE HUGE task of healing the American spirit. We have tried to diagnose and prescribe for an ailing heart, to treat the sclerotic meanness that has taken hold of our country. Now we come to wisdom and say that wisdom is a spiritual quality. But we can no more say, "Be wise," than we could say, "Have faith," or "Feel loving kindness," or "Love the stranger." All we can say is that wisdom, like faith or kindness or tolerance, is part of us, part of our tradition. We cannot tell you how not to be foolish, although each of us may have a distinct opinion. We can only tell you how to begin to be wise. Find a teacher.

Human beings learn by example. We learn from other people. We learn from books. Wisdom is not experience itself, but reflection on experience, and we can learn by reflecting on another person's experience. We associate old age with wisdom. Saint Paul said, "When I was a child, I spoke as a child, I understood as a child, I thought as a child: but when I became a man, I put away childish things." But wisdom only accompanies age when the old person has reflected on a long life's experiences. It is the quality of the reflection, not the quality of the experience, that makes for wisdom. So people can read books and grow wise. People can also grow wise sitting around a table listening to tales of cousins who ran afoul of their in-laws or of an aunt's difficult labor. There is no telling which experience or which example will prove important, so she who would be wise must listen to as much as possible. As the saying goes, a fool is one who considers all others to be fools.

By far the strongest example people have in front of them is their parents. Men and women follow the example of their parents naturally and, often, unthinkingly. Their relationships with other people are circumscribed by the types of relationships their parents had. Sometimes this is good. Sometimes this is bad. The lesson is not to admire those with lovely models and to scorn those unlucky enough to have missed the examples that would help make them wise. Wisdom lies not in the example, but in how we think about that example. Wisdom comes not from having a specific role model; it comes from our knowing that role models make a difference. That is why we don't say, "Learn and grow wise." We say, "Find a teacher."

That is precisely what thousands of children, growing up in the harshest of circumstances, do every day. They seek out reliable role models as a form of self-defense, of survival, and it works. If a boy's father is a heroin addict, he finds an uncle who is not. If a girl's house is too noisy with arguing to allow her to concentrate, she studies at her boyfriend's house. We in America are proud of our success stories. We think these survival techniques are ingenious, and we like ingenuity. We like wisdom, but we love wise guys. Street smarts. The school of hard knocks.

The burden of inventing oneself is heavy, though. As more and more Americans are foraging for their own role models and inventing their own examples, they are growing weary and bitter and mean. So let's restate our idea. We value wisdom, yes, but as a shared quality. You don't have to learn it alone. We don't just want wise Americans. We want a wise America.

There is the wisdom of the community. Together men and women have solved problems. Can we learn from their solutions? It is in this light that we look to other cultures to teach us about living on the North American continent and preserving our environment. There is the wisdom of institutions. Together men and women have built organizations to help one another. We can learn from their efforts. It is in this way that we look to America's social welfare institutions to teach us about caring for others. Finally, there is the wisdom of thousands of years of spiritual reflection. The models and examples are there, in Jesus, in the Blessed Virgin, in the saints and apostles, in Abraham and Isaac and Jacob—why not reflect on them? Join with us and we shall grow wise together.

Perhaps this book has revived your faith, in God or in America or both. If it has, it is not because we teach faith or even because we profess wisdom. Maybe it is because we have tried to show a part of America that you feared was lost, the caring, human part. We hope that this journey has prompted you to reflect, maybe in a way you don't usually reflect. The roots of Western culture are religious; our values originate in religious values. That is nothing new. It is possible, though, that you found here a link that had been missing before: a connection between big ideas and everyday behavior. What you truly believe can be reflected in your vote, your household, even in your smile. A teacher, as sober and honest as any alive, presented himself as a tutor. "What's wrong with you?" a wary parent demanded. "You don't grimace, you don't sneer, you don't squint. You don't ask me to repeat myself. You don't act like an educated person at all." A nearby listener smiled and interrupted, "That is wisdom that you see, sir. That is what wisdom looks like."

We have tried to show here a personal and human side to American religious institutions. Ours is a history of emotion, from transcendant joy so great that one's life is remade, to a single tear of sadness, so small that it is immediately lost in the cheek's fold. Sometimes the church doors look big and the edifice impenetrable. This book says that these institutions are yours. They are as strong as your courage and as weak as your despair. Love them. Care for them. We say the same for America's institutions. America is more than a piece of land. We are blessed with a people so diverse, almost anywhere you turn you can learn from your neighbors and grow wise together.

This is what we have tried to do. We have written this book together, to get to know one another better. We could have written separately. We could have followed our single traditions and argued for charity, faith, awe, and community. Together, though, our voices are stronger. We live together in an American community. We live together, Christian and Jew, black and white, rich and poor, man and woman, north and south, urban and rural, gay and straight, newcomer and first family. There are those who say otherwise. They say it is not a community and that each man, woman, and child must live and die alone. One day they will be proven wrong. One day those voices of hate will be reduced to no more than the rumblings of cranks and the whine of opportunists. Then America will live free, and the law of kindness will prevail in this land.

෨ⱳ

PATRICE DILLON WAS THE FRENCH CONSUL AT SAN Francisco during the gold fever days of the 1840s and 1850s. More amused than outraged, he wrote home of the bottomless profanity of the gold seekers who arrived daily from every port on the planet. The presence of every color, kind, and manner of human being made San Francisco the scene of comedy, drama, adventure, and escape. "I myself met a man," Dillon claimed, "not long ago secretary to a French nobleman, working as a waiter in a saloon." In short months the city sprouted venerable institutions. The University of San Francisco, Grace Church, Temple Emanu-El were all born in those days for, as Thoreau remarked at the time, "the preacher is gone to California himself."

Of all the things he saw in San Francisco, Dillon was most shocked by the scarcity of thefts. Mining gear and supplies lay totally unguarded all over the city, where a knife fight was as common as a greeting, perhaps more so. Why, he wondered, would gamblers, liars, and scoundrels of every stripe leave untouched that most precious of all commodities, the stuff of survival?

Because when it came to survival, they were all in it together.

SELECTED SOURCES

In addition to the Bible and a variety of prayerbooks, we have made use of other texts. Here are some books used in the preparation of this work which might be of interest to readers.

I. SETTING OUT

Baltzell, E. Digby, *The Protestant Establishment* (New York: Random House, 1964).

Buber, Martin, *The Legend of the Baal-Shem*, trans. Maurice Friedman (New York: Schocken, 1969).

Finkelstein, Louis, J. Elliot Ross, and William Adams Brown, *The Religions of Democracy* (New York: Devin-Adair Company, 1945).

High, Stanley, Frank Kingdon, Gerald Broveland Walsh, S.J., Louis Finkelstein, Ph.D., and Swami Nikhilananda, *Faith for Today: Five Faiths Look at the World*, with introduction and postscript by George V. Denny, Jr. (New York: Town Hall Press and Doubleday, Doran and Company, 1941).

Lipset, Seymour Martin, *Political Man* (Garden City, N.Y.: Anchor Doubleday, 1963).

Wolff, Robert Paul, Barrington Moore, Jr., and Herbert Marcuse, *A Critique of Pure Tolerance* (Boston: Beacon, 1965).

II. CROSSING PATHS

Bialik, Hayim Nahman, and Yehoshua Hana Ravnitzky, eds., *The Book of Legends: Legends from the Talmud and Midrash*, trans. William G. Braude (New York: Schocken, 1992).

Coontz, Stephanie, *The Way We Never Were* (New York: Basic, 1993).

de Tocqueville, Alexis, *Democracy in America*, trans. George Lawrence (Garden City, N.Y.: Anchor Doubleday, 1969).

Jencks, Christopher, *The Homeless* (Cambridge, Mass.: Harvard University Press, 1994).

Metzker, Isaac, ed., *A Bintel Brief: Sixty Years of Letters from the Lower East Side to the Jewish Daily Forward* (New York: Schocken, 1971).

III. CROSSING RIVERS

Bailyn, Bernard, *The Ideological Origins of the American Revolution* (Cambridge, Mass.: Belknap Press, Harvard University Press, 1967).

Catechism of the Catholic Church (New York: Doubleday, 1995).

Day, Dorothy, *Loaves and Fishes* (San Francisco: Harper and Row, 1983).

Reich, Robert, *The Work of Nations: Preparing Ourselves for 21st Century Capitalism* (New York: Vintage, 1992).

Singer, Isaac Bashevis, *Stories for Children* (New York: Farrar, Straus, and Giroux, 1984).

Vasari, Giorgio, *Lives of the Artists*, trans. E. L. Seeley (New York: Farrar, Straus, and Giroux, 1957).

IV. CLIMBING MOUNTAINS

de Chardin, Pierre Teilhard, *The Divine Milieu* (New York: Harper & Row, 1960).

Flaubert, Gustave, *Three Tales*, trans. Robert Baldick (New York: Penguin, 1961).

Galbraith, John Kenneth, *The Good Society: The Humane Agenda* (Boston: Houghton Mifflin, 1996).

Gerard Manley Hopkins, ed. the Kenyon Critics (Norfolk, Conn.: New Directions Books, 1945).

Koestler, Arthur, *Bricks to Babel* (New York: Random House, 1980).

V. THROUGH FORESTS

Clark, Kenneth, *Landscape into Art* (New York: Harper and Row, 1976).

Ricks, Christopher, and William L. Vance, eds., *The Faber Book of America* (London: Faber and Faber, 1992).

Thacker, Christopher, *The History of Gardens* (Berkeley: University of California Press, 1979).

Vasari, Giorgio, *Lives of the Artists*, trans. E. L. Seeley (New York: Farrar, Straus, and Giroux, 1984).

VI. TENDING FIELDS

Ahlstrom, Sydney E., *A Religious History of the American People*, vols. I and II (Garden City: Doubleday, 1975).

Butler's Lives of the Saints, ed. Michael Walsh (San Francisco: HarperSanFrancisco, 1991).

Hamalian, Leo, ed., *In Search of Eden* (New York: New American Library, 1981).

Kazin, Alfred, *A Lifetime Burning in Every Moment: From the Journals of Alfred Kazin* (New York: HarperCollins, 1996).

Ricks, Christopher, and William L. Vance, eds., *The Faber Book of America* (London: Faber and Faber, 1992).

VII. COUNTING SEASONS

Thomas Aquinas on Nature and Grace, trans. and ed. A. M. Fairweather (Philadelphia: The Westminster Press, 1954).

Aries, Philippe, *Centuries of Childhood,* trans. Robert Baldick (New York: Vintage, 1965.)

Bede, *A History of the English Church and People,* trans. Leo Sherley-Price (Middlesex, U.K.: Penguin, 1968).

Bier, William C., ed., *Privacy, A Vanishing Value?* (New York: Fordham University Press, 1980).

The Episcopal Diocese of California, *Vision 2000, Commission 2000 Final Report* (San Francisco: author, 1992).

Moore, Barrington, Jr., *Privacy: Studies in Social and Cultural History* (Armonk, N.Y.: M.E. Sharpe, Pantheon, 1984).

Weber, Eugen, *Peasants into Frenchmen* (Stanford: Stanford University Press, 1976).

Yerushalmi, Y., ed., *Haggadah and History: A Panorama in Facsimile of Five Centuries of the Printed Haggadah,* (New York: The Jewish Publication Society, 1975).

Zborowski, Mark, and Elizabeth Herzog, *Life Is with People: The Culture of the Shtetl* (New York: Schocken, 1952).

INDEX